RUN YOUR RACE

THE BOOK OF ACTS IS A PLAYBOOK, NOT JUST A HISTORY BOOK

CHRIS DONALD

SUPERNATURAL TRUTH PRODUCTIONS
Romulus, Michigan

SUPERNATURAL TRUTH PRODUCTIONS, LLC
Practical Training for Spirit-Filled Living
www.SupernaturalTruth.com

Copyright © 2024, Chris Donald

Run Your Race: The Book of Acts is a Playbook, Not Just a History Book

ISBN: 978-1-959547-07-5

RUN YOUR RACE

THE BOOK OF ACTS IS A PLAYBOOK, NOT JUST A HISTORY BOOK

CHRIS DONALD

ENDORSEMENT

The only thing missing in this book is the word "WARNING" on the front cover! The simple stories and practical guidance found inside will bring you to a point of decision… "Will I be reduced to just a church attending Christian my whole life or will my life matter for eternity?"

This book will take away every entrenched excuse and reason why God is not using you to change lives. You will be enticed, not condemned, to want the Holy Spirit to flow through you daily. Chris has blazed the trail, and now you can follow his simple guidance. It will change you and others around you. Enjoy the ride!

Tom Ruotolo
City Quake
www.CityQuake.org

DEDICATION

Ellie, You're beautiful inside and out. I'm so thankful that Jesus gave you to mom and me as our first child. You have taught me so much, and this book would not be what it is without the lessons that you have taught me and the stories that we have together.

ACKNOWLEDGMENTS

Sarah, thank you for taking the time to do the first edit on this book. How cool is it that it's finished, and you helped your brother write a book? You're the best!

Jay, thank you for designing the book cover and being patient as we changed it multiple times. Your artwork is beautiful. The book title was thanks to you as well. I'm so thankful to have a gifted and creative friend that helped get this book across the finish line.

Chelsea, thank you for allowing me to give everything to Jesus, day after day; and thank you for praying me through when I wanted to give up. No plan B!

// CONTENTS

// PREFACE

Over the last few years, many have asked me when I was going to write a book about my history with God. I would always give the same answer: "I will write my book when I feel that I have lived enough life to have a story worth telling and lessons worth teaching." I didn't want to just write a book for the sake of writing a book. For starters, I'm not a writer. I have always struggled with spelling and grammar, and the focus to sit and write has always escaped me. Plus, I didn't want to share principles that I had not first lived out. I want what I say and write to be authentic and true. I don't want to share or teach principles that have not been refined by fire and the trials of life. What I share with others should be truth I have walked out for a time, not just an idea that I think is cool and can help people.

I wrote this book because it's time to share with others the keys that God has given me over the past nineteen years since I've been born-again and pursued life as a full-time Christian witness. I believe that what I will share with you has the power to awaken you to live on a mission everywhere you go.

Why should you read this book? Because God needs you to be activated into a life of radical obedience to him. The harvest is ripe and ready, but the laborers are few. The people of God are stuck behind barriers and lies that are keeping them from living in the fullness of Christ.

Let's break off the lies and get you activated in being the witness Jesus has called you to be.

1

THE BOOK OF ACTS IS
A PLAYBOOK

If we are not careful, we can read the Bible, and think, *man, this is a great story of what God has done throughout history.* We can attend Bible studies and talk about what God did in the past and study these movements with great passion. Don't get me wrong, I love Bible studies and discussions about any book in the Bible. That is my passion as well. But I fear that in our Bible studies, we have turned the Bible into more of a history book than a way for us to live out what Jesus has called us to today.

The Bible is a complete book. Nothing will ever be added or taken away from it. It is the perfect Word of God, and I base my entire life on the Bible. But I also understand that the story of the Bible is not finished. From one generation to the next, the race continues as the baton is passed.

You see, the race is not over until Jesus returns. The same race that the fathers of our faith, Abraham, Isaac and Jacob, ran is not complete. Not only that, but they are cheering you on right now from heaven, hoping that you will run your race well. The same race that Peter, John, and Paul ran is the same race that you are running. The story continues today. The same fire that fell at

Pentecost is the same fire that wants to fall on your life so that you will carry the baton and pass it on to the next generation.

It is extremely important that you understand your place in God's big story. We have been so sucked into the routines of life and just trying to make it to church on Sunday in one piece that we have failed to realize that we are living in the most incredible story ever told. We are called to carry the fire to the next generation. Every time I talk about this, I feel the presence of God. Take some time to think about it. The book of Acts is so much more than just a history book; it's a playbook for us to live out today. We can heal the sick, cast out demons, preach the gospel, and disciple new believers. Not only can we do these things, but we *need* to do them. It is part of being a normal Christian.

If you want to be a sideline Christian, I would encourage you to take this book and put it back on the shelf. But if you want to be a Christian who truly steps into all that God has for you, a Christian who will one day stand before God and hear the Lord say, "Well done, good and faithful servant," then keep reading (Matthew 25:23). I want to warn you, though, that we are going to go after it in the pages that follow and many of your excuses and distractions that keep you from living out your faith daily for all to see will be exposed. There is no more exciting way to live than to see what is in the Bible unfold before your very eyes. Take the following as an example.

A few months ago, while I was at Belong, a new believer gathering, there was a young woman who had just been saved the week before. As we broke into discipleship groups, she began to express to us that she was not feeling well and just felt off. It was not a physical off, but something spiritual was off. She could not fully put into words what was happening. We began to pray for her, and suddenly her head went backward, her face contorted, and she began to growl. Yes, this is a true story. She continued growling as her body contorted. I looked at her boyfriend and calmly said, "Have you ever seen this before?"

He said no, so I explained that this was a demon, and it needed to be cast out. I then looked at my team that gathered around her and we began to pray softly and with confidence in Jesus's name. After about sixty seconds of praying, the evil spirit came out, and she was delivered. The same power the disciples were given in Acts is the same power we have today. The book of Acts, again, is a playbook for us to follow.

Ask yourself for a moment, what you would have done in this situation? Run away? Called 911? Do you even believe that demons need to be cast out today? Would you have prayed and cast it out? Unfortunately, many in the church would not have known what to do because they are not equipped. Many don't even understand that we are living in a spiritual reality. "For we do not wrestle against flesh and blood, but against the rulers, against the authorities, against the cosmic powers over this present darkness, against the spiritual forces of evil in the heavenly places" (Ephesians 6:12).

My hope is that this book will open your eyes to see that you are truly a part of something so much bigger than yourself. You are a part of the kingdom of God. My prayer is that God will use this book to awaken you to see your purpose here on earth. Are you ready to go on a journey? Are you ready to see the book of Acts play out in your everyday life? I know you are, which is why you have this book in your hands.

It's time, then, to let the book of Acts become our playbook. It's time to be baptized in the Holy Spirit (Acts 1:5). To receive power from God and be witnesses to the ends of the earth (Acts 1:8). To heal the sick (Acts 5:12–16). To spend time with Jesus and walk in boldness (Acts 4:13) To let others know what they must do to be saved (Acts 16:31). The lost, hurting, and broken are waiting for you. Take Madison, for example. Here is her story.

One Wednesday afternoon in Waco, Texas, our small team, consisting of a handful of our Jesus Year Evangelists, was joined by a group of four guys who came to learn how we do outreach and discipleship. We prayed together at the Mercy Culture Waco Church, as we normally do, before we went into the city to share the gospel with people. We always pray five specific prayers:

- That we would be led by the Holy Spirit
- That the atmosphere would shift and change around us
- That chains would break
- That God would fill the nets
- That God would send out laborers

After we prayed, we went out in faith, expecting God to answer the prayers that we had just prayed. Our team walks in such confidence because we have consistently seen the Lord show up after we pray and then step out in faith and go for the one. I think this is where many Christians miss it; they pray, but then they do not put action to their faith and expect God to answer their prayers with tangible results that same day.

That particular day, I was paired up with AJ as an outreach partner. We were in the middle of a church-wide fast, so we decided to stop at Jamba Juice for lunch as we started our outreach. At the counter, the young man behind the register was counting money and did not look up for over two minutes. As we stood there waiting for him to eventually acknowledge us, I thought we should just leave because the service was so bad. On top of that, the doors had been left open for a while, and the hot Texas air from outside had filled the store where we waited.

But the Holy Spirit told me to slow down and just wait patiently. The young man eventually took our order, and then we waited much longer than normal to get our drinks. Despite all this, I felt peace the whole time, knowing that God was somehow in this situation.

When we finally left the shop, we felt led by the Spirit to walk toward a strip mall that was a few hundred feet away. As we were walking, I looked up, and Madison was walking toward us. I knew by the Holy Spirit that she was the one that we were delayed for. She will tell you the rest of the story from her perspective.

> Growing up, my family told me I was Baptist, but I would go to Catholic schools and sometimes Pentecostal churches on the weekends. So I did not really understand what I was or where I fit in, but I knew God was real. As I got older, I was living my life how I wanted to, going to parties and doing some drugs. I lost my first boyfriend to a car accident and then my high school sweetheart to gun violence. To make matters worse, my best friend died from a drug overdose. My life was messed up. I started drinking way more than I used to and doing heavier drugs to cope with the pain. I ended up getting pregnant with my two babies during the years where I

lost my loved ones but even that did not change my life. I kept living how I wanted, thinking I was living my best life, but I was wrong. God still had something better for me.

I eventually ended up losing my job and totaling my car on the same day. I did not know how I was going to make it. I needed to stay in the state of Texas because I could make a better living than in other states. I also could not go back home to Mississippi. The very next day, while I was walking around trying to figure life out, I ran into Pastor Chris and his friend AJ. They heard a voice (Holy Spirit) telling them to find me, and they did just that. I did not want to talk to anybody, but they stopped me and asked if there was anything in my life I needed prayer for. I just broke down in tears. That's when Pastor Chris asked me if I wanted to be born again. I had nothing to lose. It was time for me to walk with God and do life his way.

At that very moment, I prayed with them, and I was born again. I then got into a van with Chris and about five or six other strangers (which our parents always teach us not to do). Getting in that van, though, was the best decision I ever made. I was brought into a family that loves me and wants me to know God. My entire life started to change that day. Later that week, I got a brand-new car and a better job. I was able to stay in Texas with my newfound family and friends. I am proud to be able to stand in faith in the Lord now. To follow the Word of God, to truly know what it means to be loved by God and to know I am his daughter.

As I read Madison's story, I'm in tears. What if AJ and I had not prayed? What if we had not been sensitive to the Holy Spirit speaking? What if we would have gotten upset, left the smoothie shop and driven somewhere else? What if we had not gone on the outreach in the first place? I do not want to live full of what-ifs, especially when it comes to doing what Jesus told every believer to do. I want to live in God's presence and fulfill His purpose. It brings me such hope and joy when Madison, along with many others like her, come into the kingdom of God. This is what Paul expressed in 1 Thessalonians 2:19–20.

> After all, what gives us hope and joy, and what will be our proud reward and crown as we stand before our Lord Jesus when he returns? It is you! Yes, you are our pride and joy. (NLT)

Yes, Paul's joy and his crown were the people that God used him to reach and disciple. Oh, how I wish that the church would understand the joy of being used by God to reach people and bring them into the kingdom of God. My sister Madison is such a joy to our community of believers. Madison's story fuels us to move forward and go after all God's sons and daughters who are crying out to know him. Are you going to join the story and step into the life God is calling you into? Yes, you are!

In the next few chapters, I'm going to share my testimony so you understand that I am just a normal person. There is nothing about my life that elevates me above anyone else. I'm simply an everyday believer that believes God at his Word and puts action to my faith. My hope is that my testimony will give you faith to believe that God will do the same through you. God will use you the same way he will use me. I know myself, and there is no way that what has happened to me was possible without God's grace. If you need proof of this, just ask my mother and wife; they will be the first to tell you I'm just a weak man who trusts in a strong God.

2

EARLY YEARS

I want to share my story so that you can understand why I write the way that I do and why I have the perspective that I do. Oftentimes, it's hard to receive from somebody when you don't really know their story or history with God. Up until this point, I have never taken the time to write down my testimony. I have shared it hundreds if not thousands of times, both one on one, and while preaching: in China, Japan, Iraq, Pakistan, Africa, Romania, Canada, Mexico, Israel, Haiti, the Philippines, and many other nations. I have shared it so many times, my oldest daughter, Ellie, has it memorized. And one of the main reasons that I'm so excited about recording it is so that my grandchildren and great grandchildren can know what happened to their grandpa. I want to leave a legacy. I want my son and daughters and grandkids to live their lives fully for Jesus. I want them to understand that we are in a spiritual battle and that even though I grew up in a Christian home and had a decent childhood, I had to have demons cast out of me at age eighteen. Keep reading for the whole story.

I was born and raised in Woodland, a small town in southwest Washington, just across the Columbia River. I still have such a heart for my hometown. I miss it very much and have so many wonderful memories of growing up on the dairy farm and playing with all my cousins all summer long. I can still hear the sprinklers used to water the cow pastures in the summer, feel the sun on my arms in July, and remember the smile that would spring to my face. When the sun comes out in Woodland, everybody smiles because fall, winter, and spring can be very wet and cloudy. The farm where I grew up was in the Woodland Valley or what we would call the Woodland Bottoms. The mouth of the Lewis River flows into the Columbia River just a few miles from where my parents' house still is to this day. When people ask me where home is I instantly think of their house surrounded by green fields and tall oak trees.

One night, at four or five years old, I was on the top bunk in my bedroom. I was about to go to bed. The lights outside the house were streaming into the bedroom through the thin blue blinds. I became aware of my need for Jesus. I don't know if it was a Sunday school class at church or a conversation that I overheard that week, but I was very sensitive to God that night. At the time, I didn't know about the Holy Spirit, but thinking back, I know it was him. I told my mom what I was feeling, and she prayed with me. When she left the room, I was overwhelmed with God's presence. God pursues us our entire lives, and at a very young age, he was revealing himself to me.

My dad and mom, David and Julie, were great parents, and I was raised in a godly home. I had an older brother and sister, Matt and Sarah, and a younger brother, Luke. I didn't know what it was at the time, but when I was in middle school and high school, I had the fear of the Lord. Maybe I had a little bit of the fear of my parents as well. But I knew right and wrong and had a very strong consciousness of God. Looking back, the Holy Spirit was with me and was often convicting me. I tried to ignore that later on, but in middle school and high school I was, in a sense, scared of drugs and alcohol. Thank God, that was the case because I never battled with drug or alcohol addiction.

My parents attended a church in town that loved God and truly preached the gospel and did all that they did unto the Lord. Just a few things were lacking in the church's theology, and one of those was the baptism in the Holy Spirit. Just to clarify, I don't think that you have to speak in tongues to go to heaven. In addition, a lot of charismatic and Pentecostal churches lack foundational elements in their theology as well. But when a believer receives the baptism in the Holy Spirit and the gift of speaking in tongues, they are empowered by the Spirit to live in victory and to do what Jesus has called us to do.

My church experience as a child until the eighth grade was at this church. I have many great memories of family church camp, Sunday potlucks, and Vacation Bible School (VBS). VBS was fun and not boring old-people church. I love it. Growing up, I really struggled with reading. In Sunday School as a seventh and eighth grader, I was afraid that I would be asked to read out of the Bible. To make it even worse, at that time, the church was a King James Version–only church, meaning that was the only version of the Bible that they read on Sundays. If you don't know what the King James Version (KJV) Bible is, check it out. The writing is in old English, similar to Shakespeare. As if reading in today's English weren't hard enough, the thought of reading old English made me all the more fearful. Some of our Sunday School teachers had everybody read a verse from the passage of the Bible that we were studying. I would count around the table so that I could guess what verse I would be asked to read. Even if I got it right and was able to look at it for a few minutes to try to figure out what it said, I would still stutter my way through it while my cousin Ben would tell me the words that I couldn't read and I would repeat them. So I didn't have much excitement when it came to the Bible. I really didn't understand it. Some of it was just because I was a young kid at the time.

In the church world during my middle school years, the Left Behind series about the rapture came out. According to those books, those who were not truly following God would be left behind to go through the tribulation, which was basically hell on earth. One week, during Sunday School, they rolled the tv cart into the room, turned off the lights, and played one of the movies. Honestly, I struggled with fear from that movie until I was probably a sophomore in high school. From the time that I watched the movie until I was in high school, my thoughts about God follow: *God is real, I think. I hope when he comes back to take the church out [the rapture], I'm lucky enough to be at church because unless I'm at church, I'll be doing something I shouldn't be doing, and I'll miss the rapture.*

One day, I was out in the field by myself in the cottonwoods, a piece of farm land right next to the railroad tracks full of cottonwood trees. I was asked at work that day to pick tansy, a plant poisonous to cattle, so that the farm horses or cattle would not eat it and get sick. The whole time I was out there, I hoped that my family would still be there when I got home. I'm not exaggerating. If the church talked about having a relationship with God, I missed it. I don't ever remember hearing that I could know God personally and that I didn't need to live in fear. I don't remember hearing about the secret place and that having a relationship with God was an amazing experience. Again, I was young, so that could have all gone over my head. Later on, I went to Bible college and learned that the word *rapture* is not even in the Bible and that those books and movies took verses completely out of context. I was shocked and relieved at the same time.

When I transitioned into high school, my parents made a big decision to leave the church that I grew up in and start going to a new church, the Ridgefield Church of the Nazarene. They still attend this wonderful community church today. This was a huge decision and came with a cost to step away from the church they grew up in. As I said, I had grown up attending church, but when we switched churches, I could sense something was different there. I didn't know what it was, but I could sense life. Looking back now, it was the Holy Spirit once again.

I attended Woodland High School, and my passion was basketball. I also enjoyed track and field and ran cross country just to stay in shape for basketball. I was not the most athletic kid but was athletic enough to make the JV basketball team and then move up to varsity my junior and senior years. In middle school, I was undefeated in the 110-meter hurdles, but in high school, the hurdles were higher, and the competition grew more intense. My senior year, I was back on top in hurdles at school and at district, but then, it was time to graduate. For me, like for many teenagers, high school had its ups and downs with hormones and puberty thrown in there.

My biggest challenge in high school was an on-again, off-again dating relationship that honestly took a lot of the joy out of school. In middle school, all I was thinking about was basketball, other sports, and hanging out with the boys. One day, at lunch, I was playing basketball with my friends, and a group of girls that I really didn't even know walked out on the floor and asked me if I would date this girl. I didn't even know who she was. What was I thinking? I agreed to date a girl that I never met, which was the start of five years of turmoil that really brought a lot of compromise into my life. She didn't have a dad and was not brought up in a Christian home. She wasn't a bad person but was broken like we all are before Jesus. I was young and driven by my flesh, having really no understanding of what I was doing. My sinful nature, feelings, and thoughts were in the driver's seat. It was awful. I was a slave to sin and didn't even know it.

In high school, I ended up losing my virginity to her, which made the relationship all the more complicated. One compromise led to another, and compromise has a high price tag. I didn't know what I was getting myself into until it was too late. I had lived a rather sheltered life. We didn't watch rated R movies and definitely didn't cuss. Even the word *butt* was off limits in our house. Once I crossed certain boundaries, it was all downhill from there. I started lying to my parents and doing things that I had never done before, all with God in the back of my mind.

One of the many times that we broke up, I told my friend Casey that I was not going to get back together with her and if I did, he could punch me. (I'll share more about him later.) I could take you to the very hall where he punched me. I was shocked that he actually did it, but I did go back on my word. I was hooked because I crossed a boundary that I never should have and was stuck with really no way out. After I was born again, I talked with her over the phone and apologized for what I had done in that relationship. My eyes were opened to see my blindness, which made me aware of the hurt that I had caused her. I was also able to tell her about Jesus and what he did for me by setting me free. I led her in a prayer to start a relationship with him. I don't know what that prayer led to, but I do know that God takes bad situations and turns them to good.

In high school, I encountered God three times. He was coming after me, and I really didn't even know that it was him until after I was saved at age eighteen. The first encounter was at a church that my brother Matt and sister-in-law Kim were going to in Vancouver, Washington. My girlfriend and I were at church with them for a Saturday night service. They did communion during worship, and you had to go down front to get the cup and bread. I just did what everybody else was doing and went down front too. The Holy Spirit encountered me, and I couldn't stop crying as a deep feeling come on me. He was convicting me of how I was living.

After church, I got in the car with my girlfriend and told her I didn't know what that was, but I thought I need to start living better. I told her we needed to stop sleeping together, but that didn't last long. To me, church was a list of rules that you followed to make God and your parents happy. I didn't understand that I could truly be born again and be filled with the Holy Spirit. I was defenseless against the attacks of the enemy and my own sinful flesh. I was just being tossed around all over the place.

The next encounter that I had with God was later that year at my friend Andrew Larson's youth group in Vancouver, Washington. One Wednesday night, I visited that youth group for the first and only time. (Not because I didn't like it but it was a long drive from Woodland.) This was one of the first churches where I experienced contemporary worship with lights and a fog machine. I was sitting in the middle section of chairs just taking it all in: the blue and purple lights and the loud music and the multiple singers on the stage. As I was looking at a man holding a microphone on the stage, a voice spoke to me. "You are going to do that." I had no desire to ever do that and just pushed that voice out of my mind as quickly as I heard it. But that stuck with me for the next few years. It was not my voice or thoughts because I would never think that way. God was showing me what he had planned for me.

The last encounter I had with God before my major life-changing encounter was right after I graduated from high school one Sunday morning at the Nazarene church. The rule in our house was if friends stayed over on Saturday night, they had to go to church on Sunday morning with the family. I never argued about that or tried not to go to church; it was just the way it was. So this particular Sunday, my friend Patrick from Sweden was with me at church. He was a foreign exchange student and was just along for the ride.

The service that week was different; they acted out a sermon analogy in the service. A woman walked down the aisle in a wedding gown. Every few steps she took, something happened to her and the gown: rips, stains, and a mess, all to represent what happens in our lives before Jesus. When she reached the stage, she had a moment with God where she was given a new dress and was restored to better than before.

Patrick and I both lost it, crying. Again, something very deep was happening in my heart, but I didn't know what it was. As soon as church was out, we left. It was a sunny summer day, so we jumped in my Chevy Lumina, which was maroon inside and out. My grandparents had given it to me, and I had put spinner hubcaps on it. We started driving to Papa Pete's Pizza, our favorite spot. On our way, we both kind of looked at each other. We didn't know what had happened, so we just went about our day, living the same way as before. I talked to my friend Patrick years later, and like me, he still remembers that day that God touched us both.

The Nazarene church gave all the high school graduates, including me, a nice big navy-blue Bible. I left it in my room and didn't really pay any attention to it because I didn't understand it and was not passionate about reading it at all. By this time, I was fully in the world.

After high school, I needed to figure out what I was doing with my life. Farming wasn't really an option. At one point, my dad said to my brothers and me that we needed to find something else to do because the farm wasn't doing as well as it did when he was younger. He was right because a few years ago, they closed down the dairy part of the farm.

I had always wanted to be a police officer, and one day, I was talking to my uncle Mike, who served as a Longview policeman for many years. He said, "You should be a fireman. Everybody likes firemen, but not everybody likes cops." So that was it—I decided to pursue a career as a fireman. I joined the volunteer fire department and enrolled in a Fire Science program at a local community college.

In my first Fire Science class, the instructor said to us, "You don't have to be in this class to be a fireman." So I dropped the class because if I didn't have to go to school, that was even better. the department that I volunteered for sent me to a fire academy. I passed. Then I took an EMT course and passed that as well. To me, that was a big deal because I always struggled with book work and testing. I really enjoyed the excitement of firefighting and helping people, so it was a great fit. I was really excelling in the department and had favor with the paid firefighters. They believed that if I kept going, I would be hired in a paid position in the next few years.

During this season, I began to live a little more on the edge. I started drinking more, partying and became heavily addicted to pornography to the point where it began to destroy my life and relationships. I met a girl that lived across the river, and we began to date. I was a jerk and completely consumed with lust. At the same time, I was talking to other girls and living out of control.

One day, my friends woke me up and surrounded me in my friend Jonathan's apartment. They started kicking and punching me, telling me to stop being an idiot. They knew that I was not being a faithful boyfriend. They all liked my current girlfriend and were telling me to get my act together. So I decided to change and told them that I would no longer be talking to other girls. In my mind, I had really made the shift and was going to do what was right. But thinking back, there was no way that would have happened because I didn't have a relationship with Jesus. I was so lost.

In this season, during one of my lowest and darkest moments, I was driving in my car, completely overcome with sin and lust and looking at pornography. I felt darkness all around me. I thought, *What have I become?* I was so lost and had no way out. Romans 6:20–21 says, "For when you were slaves of sin, you were free in regard to righteousness. But what fruit were you getting at that time from the things of which you are now ashamed? For the end of those things is death."

3

LIFE-CHANGING GOD ENCOUNTER

A day after my friends confronted me, one of them called my girlfriend and told her what I had been doing. So of course, she was done. She called me and said that she was coming to my house to talk to me. I knew she was about to break up with me. When she got there, the conversation was short and she told me that she didn't want anything to do with me any longer. I started to rage and punched a hole in my downstairs bedroom wall. The patch is still on the wall to this day in my parents' house.

She left, and I was beyond upset and angry. My parents called Casey Schang, my closest childhood friend. We had known each other since third grade. He was a good influence, and his dad, Scott, was the pastor of a local church. Casey came right over and sat with me in my parents' basement. He tried to tell me about Jesus and even prayed for me. He left a few hours later. Being around him really helped me calm down. Later that night, I began to lose it again. At one point during my anger and rage in my bedroom, my dad had to physically wrestle me and hold me down so that I didn't hurt myself or the house.

The next three days were long, awful, and emotional. I was working at the dairy farm and was certain that my girlfriend would come back and want to talk, so I thought every car that drove by was maybe her. She never came back, and each day that passed just got worse and worse. On the third day, I found out that she had gotten back together with her ex-boyfriend. When I heard this news, I became so jealous and angry and was beginning to lose it again as the rage came back. I went outside, and my dad was getting back from work. I was pacing back and forth, and my dad was talking to me, trying to calm me down. I looked over toward the house, and my younger brother, Luke, was standing in the window watching me. I will never forget the look on his face. He was trying to figure out if his big brother was going to be okay.

My dad finally said, "Why don't you go inside and try reading the Bible?" So I decided to do that and went in the house and got my brand-new big navy-blue Bible. I took it into the living room and sat down to begin to read it. Luke was in bed. My dad had to go to my grandpa's house to be with him overnight. He was on a rotation with my uncles to take care of grandpa who was beginning to seriously decline in health. I opened up the Bible to begin to read, and all the words appeared blurry. I tried reading for a few minutes but couldn't focus at all. I then had the thought: *You need to go and hurt the guy that is with your girlfriend.* So I put the Bible down on the coffee table in the living room and closed it and then tried to stand up to get my keys to go and hurt him. But when I went to stand up, my hand was supernaturally stuck to the Bible. As hard as I tried, I couldn't pull my hand off the Bible. I told my mom what I was going to do, and she ran into the other room and came back and sat down in fear that I would get the keys and leave. I told my mom that if I could, I would hurt her and take the keys from her because I had to go and hurt this guy. It shifted from me to a demon that took over control of me.

My mom will tell you that my eyes rolled back in my head, and at times, another voice came out of my mouth that was not mine. A battle was taking place inside of me. A voice spoke in the pit of my stomach, a demonic spirit, and it was as if my heart somehow was connected to God. The devil and God were warring for my mind. I was completely out of control and was coming in and out of consciousness. I could talk and was aware of what was going on the whole time. It was very strange. The demon in me was trying to destroy my life. When I was young, I prayed to Jesus and asked him to save me. God was with me and was at work.

My mom called my dad, and he quickly came home from the farm less than a mile away. He walked into the house and sat by me on the couch. I looked at him and said, "I'm the devil. Let your son go do what he needs to do." He called my uncle Steve who quickly came as well to see if he could help. When he arrived, he sat next to me and prayed for me. They needed more help, so they called Pastor Scott Schang, Casey's dad. God ultimately knew that he was equipped to deal with the demonic spirit and cast it out. Earlier that week, my mom reached out to their church and couldn't reach a pastor to come and help me. They seemed to lack the urgency to help. In hindsight, God knew who was equipped to help.

My parents got out the phone book to look up his phone number, but he was not listed. They panicked a bit, trying to figure it out. I knew their phone number by heart because I was always calling Casey to hang out. All of a sudden, I could speak and blurted out the number. The moment I said the number, I lost control again, and the war continued. They quickly called the number, and Scott answered and said that he and Lori would come right over. A fun fact is that Chelsea, my future wife, was at Scott and Lori's house that night with their daughter, Destiny. She heard the phone ring and when they were leaving, she asked them where they were going. They said, "We are going to cast a demon out of Chris Donald."

After my parents hung up and told me that Scott was coming I knew that I would be freed from this thing when he got there. I don't know how I knew it, but I just did. I could talk again for a moment and said to my dad, "This thing knows that when Scott gets here, it's over. Please hold me down if I try to run away."

When Scott and Lori got to the house I thought, *What is going to happen*? This kind of thing had never happened in our family before, and the only context that I had for deliverance was a couple of horror movies that I watched. I had no clue what to expect, but what happened was the total opposite. They came in the house and sat down in front of me and simply asked, "What is allowing this thing to have a place in your life?" I quickly mentioned the pornography and alcohol in my room. Pastor Scott said that was part of it but what else was? I began to tell him about the sin in my life that had a hold on me.

After I confessed that sin to God, we went downstairs into my room with a big trash bag, and I threw all the pornography and alcohol away. Then we came back up the stairs and sat back down in the living room. The demon had calmed down and was hiding. Scott and Lori said that they were going to go back home but pray for me one last time. As they laid their hands on me to pray, the demon spoke to me again. "As soon as they leave, we are going to do what we came to do." (They meant they would hurt that guy.) I had no power to say anything. I was locked up and could not speak.

As they were praying, Pastor Lori pulled her hand off me. "It's not gone yet." I believe God truly saved my life that day because she heard the voice of God. They then asked my parents if they could pray in the Holy Spirit over me. My parents said yes, absolutely. I grew up only hearing negative things about people that spoke in tongues, but that day I was glad to have people that believed in the power of the Holy Spirit. As they began to pray in the Holy Spirit, the power of that demonic spirit broke, and I was truly delivered. They spent a little more time with us and then left. Pastor Scott accidentally left his coat at the house, but we don't think that it was an accident at all. It was hanging on the banister all night and brought comfort to my mom and me. At age eighteen, I fell asleep in my mom's arms on the couch.

The next morning when I woke up, I felt light and free, as if I was a new person. The weight and shame that I carried from my sin for the longest time were gone. I was right with God, and the demon that was trying to destroy my life was gone. The first thing that I wanted to do was empty my room out and start fresh. My grandmother, DeeAnn, and my mom helped me. We filled garbage sacks full of clothes, shoes, and other items that I needed to give away that I was attached to. Grandma took it all to Goodwill. We took all my posters off the wall and completely cleared out the room. The last thing that I had to get rid of was a New York Yankees jersey that I had bought and loved. I was on my knees with tears in my eyes, holding on to it, and my grandma said, "You just need to let it go." So I gave it to her, and she put it in one of the bags.

That night, I was sitting in an empty room with a few holes in the wall, a reminder of when I was angry. My dad came down the stairs with drywall, mud, and a trowel. I told him that I was sorry for what I did, and he said it was okay. He began to patch up the hole in my bedroom wall. That moment of love from my natural father revealed the love of my heavenly Father. Jesus is so wonderful because he truly forgives us when we repent and have godly sorrow. God used this moment to reveal his love, mercy and forgiveness to me on the first day that I was walking out my new Christian life. My dad could have easily been frustrated with me and the extra work that he had to do when patching the wall, but he wasn't upset. He was happy that his son was free. There was no condemnation or shame, only grace, mercy, and joy. It's so important that we understand this about God. This is the foundation of our relationship with our heavenly Father. I was sitting in a room that was cleaned out and fixed up. I was ready to start my new life.

"So now there is no condemnation for those who belong to Christ Jesus. And because you belong to him, the power of the life-giving Spirit has freed you from the power of sin that leads to death" (Romans 8:1–2 NLT).

4

MY CALL

Pastor Scott had mentioned that I probably needed to go to their church to continue to grow in the things of God. I didn't really want to at first, probably because most of what I had heard about that church growing up was negative. So I went to one more church service with my parents. During the meeting, I just knew in my spirit that I needed to go to Life Center Church (they later changed the name to The Promise Church).

The next week, I went, and man, what a different experience. Everybody went forward and raised their hands, and there was so much energy in the room. I went up front with Casey as his mom was leading worship. Everybody was dancing, which I had never experienced, and during the song, Lori looked and me and said, "Come on Chris, dance." I started dancing and felt such incredible freedom in my spirit. This was one of the first times that I truly experienced the joy of worship.

The church believed in the baptism in the Holy Spirit, and all my new church family was excited for me to receive it and to also speak in tongues. I was not raised around that, so I was a bit scared. I was open, but I said all the time, when people prayed for me, "I'm not going to fake it until I make it. If it's God, it will happen."

During the first few months after my encounter with God, I basically lived at Casey's church apartment. On a few occasions, when I stayed at the firehouse, Casey came over and prayed for me. One night, I was sitting in Casey's gray Jeep Wrangler as he prayed for me to receive the baptism of the Holy Spirit and to speak in tongues. Nothing happened that I could tell. But every time we pray, something happens. God was just chipping away the religion that I had been brought up in, along with the lies that the things of the Spirit are not for all believers today.

Three months after I was saved, the youth group was taking a trip to a youth conference in Seattle. I had never been to a church conference before, so I was excited to see what it was all about. The conference was being held at Lakeland Church and seated ten thousand people. We got there a bit late due to traffic, so our youth group was seated in the overflow room with a few hundred other people where we watched the service on a screen. The speaker that night was T.D. Jakes from Dallas. As he began to speak, I was captivated by his message about David and Goliath. Toward the end of the message, he stopped. "The Holy Spirit is here. Turn and give somebody a hug."

I turned to Pat West, a friend from The Promise Church, and before I knew it, I was flat on my back, screaming in tongues. That's right, screaming. The Holy Spirit came on me. Everything in my life was about to change. While I was on the ground, the voice of God said, "You are going to travel the world, heal the sick, cast out demons, raise the dead, cleanse the lepers, and preach the gospel." It was so loud in my spirit that it was as if it were the audible voice of God.

When I stood up, I began to tell everybody what I was going to do: travel the world, preach the gospel, and change the world for Jesus. The funny thing was that for the first year, I thought I would be just like the Bishop T.D. Jakes, suit and all, because that is who I saw when I was called. When we made it back to the hotel room, I got in bed and couldn't stop praying in the Holy Spirit. I was baptized in the Holy Spirit and called, all in the same moment.

I want to share a few relevant points here. I never wanted to be in ministry. That was never a thought in my mind until I had this encounter with God, and he spoke to me. Also, I had never read the Bible up to this point, so when the Lord spoke to me about what I was going to do for him, all that was new to me. I didn't know this was even possible. I spent the first year or so after I was filled with the Holy Spirit reading the Bible and seeing that everything he spoke to me that day was in the Bible and was what we as believers were called to do.

I want to say this as lovingly as I can but still have it pack a punch. I don't care if you like me or agree with me about this. I had an encounter with Jesus, and he spoke to me and then showed me in the Word to confirm that this is what we are called to do. I'm telling you my story so that you can understand that I'm not moved by man but by God. It's my job to help equip the church to do what Jesus has called us to do. I'm not a professional preacher or pastor; I'm just a kid who grew up on a dairy farm and had an encounter with God. I'm going to tell the whole world about it no matter who likes it.

When we got back to town, I sat in Pastor Scott's office and shared the whole experience with him. He quickly came to the conclusion that I needed to go to Bible college. I agreed, and before you know it, I signed up for Portland Bible College (PBC). I wasn't going to be a fireman, so I shared with the department that I was quitting. The main fireman that worked with us on shift tried very hard to talk me out of it. "You are making a big mistake. You are good at what you do and are close to getting a paid job." I said very matter-of-factly that I was quitting, so in one final effort to scare me out of it, he told me that I had to share my story with all the firemen in the department on a training night.

I agreed and that Tuesday night came when I was going to speak. About eighty people were in the room. I got up and shared in fear and trembling. This was the first time that I had shared my testimony in front of people, so you can imagine it was very raw. I'm sure that it put a smile on Jesus's face. "I'm going to be quitting the fire department so that I can go to Bible college. I had an encounter with God, and he told me that I was going to heal the sick, cast out demons, raise the dead, cleanse the lepers, and preach the gospel. And when God spoke to me, he also baptized me in the Holy Spirit, and I speak in tongues." That was about it. I'm sure they thought I was crazy, but many of them have watched my journey and have realized it was God.

Right before Bible college started, I was at our church's youth camp and a special guest speaker was there, Derrill Corbin. During the ministry time, he gave me a prophetic word. I had never experienced the prophetic before. He said that in five years, a man would come to our church like Paul came to Timothy in Acts 16 and ask me to travel with him. That word was exciting, but five years is a long time when you're nineteen. But I held that word in my heart and started Bible college. On the first day, Glenda Malmin, the women's dean, gave me a prophetic word in the first class of the year. She said many different things that confirmed what pastor Derrill and the Lord had said to me that night that I was baptized in the Holy Spirit. She said I would be a sign and wonder to a generation and that I would travel the world with a fivefold apostolic company. We would be an army of deliverance used by the Lord. It was another word that marked my life deeply. I was so hungry for God that I was taking it all in.

I had to get a new job because the farm hours didn't work well with Bible college hours, so I started working for Rain City, a pressure washing company in Vancouver, Washington. I got up at 5:00 a.m., drove to school to be there by 7:15 a.m., got out at noon or 1:00 p.m. and drove to work. It was such a fun season.

God began to teach me that he is a provider. The second semester of school, I went to sign up for classes and only had two dollars to my name. They said that they really felt that I was called to be at PBC, so they gave me an extension to make my first payment. After enrolling that day, I went to work, and John Day, the owner of the company, asked me to come into his office for a moment. He asked me how school was going, and I said great. He then asked me how my school payments were going, and I said great. He knew that wasn't the truth, so he asked me again, and I told him that I just signed up that day for the next semester with two dollars. John then pulled out his checkbook and paid for the next two years of my Bible school tuition. John is now with the Lord. I preached at his funeral, which was an absolute honor. He was used in a major way to sow into my life at the beginning.

If you had asked me in that season what I was going to do with my life, I would have told you I was going to travel the world and preach the gospel. I attended Portland Bible College for two years and, by the grace of God, graduated with honors with my associate's degree in theology. My mother said she always knew I was smart. I just needed to find what I was interested in, and when I found God, I found that very thing. Our church then started a school of supernatural ministry that I attended and then began leading by helping with outreaches and equipping.

During this season, I fell in love with my wife and best friend Chelsea. She was still in high school when we first met at church. She had a decision to make when she was choosing which high school to attend, and I'm so happy she chose Woodland High School. When she was in third grade, her family had moved from San Diego to a piece of property in View, Washington, that her parents had inherited from Jim's mother, Grandma Diana. To this day, she is one of Chelsea's most favorite people. I could not meet her before she passed away, but Chelsea assures me that she would have loved me.

View is located twenty minutes east of Woodland in the foothills. The drive from Woodland to View is, to this day, one of my favorites. It's so beautiful as the road winds its way through the tall evergreens and follows the Lewis River as it travels up toward View, Amboy, Yacolt, and eventually, to the base of Mount Saint Helens. Chelsea attended Green Mountain School from third through eighth grade. The tiny school was only a few miles from the family property in Amboy. Her class size was eight kids. Green Mountain didn't have a high school, so the students in that district could choose from multiple schools. Her brothers all chose La Center High School, but Chelsea decided to go to Woodland because she had met the basketball coach and wanted to play for a strong basketball team. Looking back now, the providence of God led her to Woodland.

Chelsea met Destiny Schang, Pastor Scott's daughter, who played on the basketball team with her. Destiny invited Chelsea to church, and she was baptized in the Holy Spirit at a youth summer camp. When I met Chelsea, she was on fire for God. One of the first times I saw her was at the church shop one night when Casey and I were building a skate ramp for a youth event. She was standing on a skateboard. I thought, *Who is this girl? She is cute.*

Chelsea and I began to build a friendship from that point on. We all practically lived at the church during that season: from prayer nights throughout the week, Friday night worship, and church on Sunday. We went to church almost every day. As our friendship grew, we exchanged phone numbers and began to call each other most nights to talk about what God had done that day. One night, I was sitting in front of the firehouse on a park bench talking with Chelsea on the phone. When I hung up, I thought about how much I enjoyed talking to her and that I would like to date her. Around that same time, she said she could tell that I began to like her because I always texted her to make sure that she made it home safely.

When our romantic interest in each other became evident, what happened next is one of my favorite parts of the story. Chelsea asked me to go outside the church to talk for a few minutes. I sat down on the picnic table as she stood there. "Listen, I like you, and you seem to like me. There is one thing you need to know. If you are going to like me, then I'm the only person you can like." She laid it out plain and simple. I was smart enough to agree and let her know my feelings.

I was known to be quite the player in high school. The first time she heard my name, the girls on the high school basketball team were talking about me. Chelsea wanted to make sure that I would stop that. After this high moment of sharing our feelings for one another, though, came a low moment in our relationship. Our church youth group was very strict about dating and quite religious in that area. A youth leader had challenged me to not date for a year or two, and I agreed to do that out of zealousness to please God. I made an oath that I should not have made. So after telling each other that we had feelings for one another, Chelsea and I made a decision to actually not talk for a whole year, which was really stupid, looking back at it.

During that year, I would drive into the church parking lot, and if Chelsea's car was there, my heart would race because I could see her from a distance. Our church at that time was only a few hundred people, so you couldn't really hide from anybody. One of the church mommas knew that we liked each other and scheduled us to work in the nursery together during that year. I'm not going to lie, that was the best part of my church experience that year because I got to be in the same room as Chelsea.

Thankfully, my new friend, Robbie, who had moved to town to pursue a relationship with Destiny, came along at just the right time. One night at prayer, he talked to me and helped me break free from the weird oath I had made. That night, he walked me over to Chelsea, who was praying by the usher's closet. I sat down and began to talk to her. We started dating that week, got engaged one year later, and married four months after our engagement. We have been married for fifteen years as of the writing of this book and now have four beautiful children. Where did the time go? Chelsea is the greatest gift that God has ever given me, and I am realizing more and more each year how blessed I am to have a wife that loves God and fears the Lord. She is truly a Proverbs 31 woman.

In between Bible college and the prophetic word that I was holding onto about a man coming to our church and asking me to travel the world with him, I worked a lot of different jobs: on the dairy farm, in a feed store, for a pressure washing company, and in construction work. During those five years, no matter where I was working, if you asked me what I was going to do with my life, I would have told you I was going to travel the world and preach the gospel. There was no Plan B. God had spoken, and I was all in on what he said. And once I married Chelsea, I had the best encourager in the world on my side. A few times, I wanted to quit and get a normal career job because I was watching all my friends grow up, get great jobs, and buy houses. I really had nothing but a word from God. Chelsea told me, "No, that's not what God said. You are going to do something great for God." Like I said, I would not be here today without my wife and her constant belief in me and what God said to both of us.

We hosted a conference at our church and invited Chad Dedmon from Bethel Church to come and share with us. He was gifted in hearing God and evangelism, and our church was really moving in that direction. Before one of the sessions, during worship, he looked at me. "Hey, do you and your wife want to travel with me to Africa?" My response was yes, but I told him that we didn't have the money and would need to figure that part out. He said okay and was confident the money would come in.

And it did! That night, I called my aunt Patty, who is a missionary and a big part of my life. I told her what happened, and she said that she would bless us with the money and gave us more than enough to go on the trip.

That next week, we realized that the prophecy had come true. It had been five years since the prophetic word to the month because we always held youth camp (now a youth conference) in that month. The prophetic word came true, and the door opened to the nations, and we walked through it. Since that door has opened, we have been to more than twenty-five nations preaching the gospel.

Chelsea's and my journey has not been without trials. We have had moments of pain, disappointment, loss, persecution, false accusations, and just normal life pressures. But over and over, we have chosen to say yes to Jesus and to his call to make disciples. Our motivation to keep going in the midst of pain and discomfort has been that God has saved us both and called us for a purpose. Our motivation to continue to advance the kingdom of God is that he first loved us. Wherever you are in your God journey, continue to say yes to Jesus because he is worthy.

5

STEPPING INTO MY CALL AS AN EVANGELIST

When Kevin Dedmon came to our church, he brought a team of students with him—a "fire team" from Bethel Supernatural School of Ministry (BSSM). The first night that he was preaching, he was sharing about Lonnie Frisbee, an evangelist who was used by God powerfully in the 1970s during the Jesus People movement. He had a gift of miracles and a word of knowledge that was very strong on his life. God had chosen to use this very interesting man to start two major church movements: Calvary Chapel and the Vineyard. He struggled in his life and ministry for a time but was right with God by the end of his life. There was no question that God used him powerfully. As Kevin was talking about him and the mantle that he carried from God, I began to see something around Kevin. I can best describe it as if a mirage were fully surrounding him. The definition of a *mirage* is "an optical illusion caused by atmospheric conditions, especially the appearance of a sheet of water in a desert or on a hot road caused by the refraction of light from the sky by heated air."[1]

I squeezed my eyes together a few times, thinking they were playing tricks on me, but I looked around the room and saw everything else just fine. When I looked back at Kevin, all I could see was a mirage around him to the point that I could no longer see him, just what was around him. I was sitting next to Pastor Scott, and I asked him if he saw it but he didn't seem to see what I was seeing. I probably sounded crazy. The mirage came off Kevin and landed on me, which I could physically feel. It was the mantle that Lonnie carried for evangelism. At the time, I knew nothing about mantles or impartation, so I didn't really know what took place. But looking back, knowing what I know now, that was a spark that launched me on a journey of sharing my faith. The gift of word of knowledge began to operate in my life powerfully.

The next day, the fire team took us on an outreach. I had never done anything like this before. I had shared my story with people and talked to friends and family about Jesus but had never approached a stranger and talked to them about Jesus. I was slightly nervous but was paired up with Pastor Dan, Sarah Taylor, and a girl from the fire team. We drove in Dan's car toward downtown Woodland. Right when we turned onto the main road, the girl with us asked us to stop so she could talk to someone. Dan pulled the car over, and she jumped out and chased down a person walking down the street. I was blown away by her lack of fear. Watching her step out in boldness boosted my faith. Then, it was my turn. We stopped at a store and got out, and I shared my faith for the first time in public. Something broke open in my life in that moment. It was like I knew that this was what I was created for.

After the fire team went back to Bethel, the fire for evangelism never went out. I started sharing with people all the time and began to hear God's voice more consistently through the word of knowledge. The first time that I got a word of knowledge was at Pro Caliber Motorsports in Vancouver, Washington. I was

---

[1] *The Oxford Pocket Dictionary of Current English*, "mirage," Encyclopedia.com, accessed November 17, 2024, https://www.encyclopedia.com/humanities/dictionaries-thesauruses-pictures-and-press-releases/mirage-0.

in the section of the store that sold Motocross jerseys when, all of a sudden, I felt a warm hand touch my back. I turned around to see who had touched me, and nobody was there except for a guy across the store. I thought it must have been a word of knowledge and thought, *Well, let's give this a try.* I walked across the store and asked the guy if he had a bad back. He said yes. I was probably more surprised than he was. I asked if I could pray for him, and he let me pray right there in the store. These kinds of encounters continued to happen often as I was growing in the gifts God had given me.

When this first started happening, I worked at the dairy farm, mostly around family. Whenever I would see a truck driver pull onto the farm property, I ran over and asked the driver if I could pray for them and share with them that Jesus loved them.

I then had to change jobs due to Bible college and my school schedule and started working at L&J Feed store in town. Once I got all the chore work down around the shop, I sat at the front desk reading Bill Johnson books, waiting for customers. I made it a point to do my best to share Jesus with every customer that came in. It was a great job.

I met John Day at church, and he asked me if I wanted to work for him at his company Rain City, doing pressure washing. At my new job, I was around staff that didn't know Jesus, so I shared with them. I went out on a lot of job sites and always shared Jesus with the customers. One day, I was asked to come into my boss's office. He had received a letter from a customer who I had worked for, thanking him for allowing his workers to pray for people. He was encouraged by the letter and said to keep sharing.

After Bible college, I went back to work at the farm for a season and kept sharing with truck drivers. But I think the Lord knew that I needed to be around more people to continue to grow the gift of evangelism. I was out in a field one day working on a fence when my phone rang. This man, Daniel Remier, had got my number from Pastor Scott. He was looking for help at his construction business and asked if I would like to work for him. The offer sounded great. The day he called, I was lying under a barbed wire fence with a fence stretcher. This move to Remier Construction was definitely an open door from God.

Dan became a great friend, and I worked for him for close to eight years. He allowed me to travel when that door opened and really supported all that God was doing through me. Most of the time, Dan and I just worked together, but he would hire contractors as well. I was always helping him accomplish whatever needed to be done. I was a great worker with a strong work ethic, But I lacked mathematics skills and more complicated construction concepts. Even so, Dan was always very gracious with me.

In that season, the gift that I had been stewarding went to another level. I began to share with everybody all day long, and Dan allowed me to. He loved the Lord and knew that God was doing something special in my life. Once, we went to Parr Lumber in Portland, and I felt that I had a word of knowledge for a worker. I asked if he had bad knees and he said no but that he had a bad back. So I asked if I could pray for him right there in the lumber yard and he agreed. I laid hands on him and began to pray. He looked at me. "What the hell did you do to me? Are you a witch?" I explained to him that I was a Christian. He bent over, and God had completely healed his back. These kind of things began to happen more frequently, and people began to notice.

I had a conversation with Pastor Scott about what was happening and was always sharing testimonies with him. One day, in his office, I asked him why everybody else didn't do the same thing I was doing. My question wasn't judgmental but sincere, wondering why more people weren't doing outreach. His answer really sank in, and that was the first time that I realized that I was called to be an evangelist. "Chris, you need to understand that what is happening in your life is amazing. Don't stop. But not everybody will have as many stories as you do. You are growing in the office of an evangelist and not everybody is an evangelist."

It took me a few years to fully get what he was saying. I was still growing in my knowledge of Scripture and didn't fully understand what the fivefold ministry was. Pastor Scott believed that all people should share their faith and be used by God, but he recognized that the gift on my life was different. Because all I thought about was sharing Jesus with people.

One day, Dan and I were working on a job site in Portland, and an inspector came to look at the electrical and plumbing. As soon as he walked in the door of the house, I got a word of knowledge for his right foot. I waited for him to inspect the house, and as he was leaving, I caught up to him. "Excuse me, sir. When you walked into the house, the Lord spoke to me and told me that you have a bad right foot. Is that true? If so, I would like to pray for you."

His jaw dropped. I have never experienced anything like this since then. He just stared at me with a blank expression for what seemed like thirty seconds. He then just said he had to go. I could tell he was scared, so I said, "Hey, I'm just a Christian. Are you a Christian?"

He said, "Yes." I knew by the way that he was dressed he was an old apostolic Lutheran, so this was all new for him. So I said, "Just take a deep breath. This is God." I knew the word was right. After he calmed down, he shared that weekend he was riding a dirt bike and wrecked it. He totally messed up his right foot and was in a ton of pain. After I prayed for him, the pain completely left. He was so thankful and walked away with a better understanding of the love of Jesus. To many, the old apostolic church has become just a religion and not a personal relationship with God.

Another day, I was at a job site in Portland, in front of a home, removing siding. A van pulled up with a cabinet contractor in it. Normally, Dan and I would do the cabinets in a house, but on this job, the owner wanted these specific cabinets done by a friend. When he was walking up the path, I received a word of knowledge for his shoulder. By now, I could clearly hear from the Lord and obey. When he walked by me, I asked, "Hey man, sorry to bug you, but I was wondering if you have pain in your right shoulder?" He told me that he did, and then I asked if I could pray for him because God wanted to heal it.

The man said, "Not right now but talk to me later."

So I waited about five minutes for him to take his tools in the house and walked into the living room where he was working. "Can I pray for you now?" He started yelling, telling me to leave him alone. I was very honoring and said that I was sorry for bugging him and went out to the front of the house to start removing siding again. Dan wasn't there, but a countertop guy was in the kitchen and overheard what happened.

The next day on the drive to the job site, Dan shared with me that the countertop guy told him what happened. Dan was such an encouragement to me as I was growing in the gift and said that it was okay and told me not to stop sharing with people. He knew I was sensitive and had solid people skills, so he trusted me. He knew I was a great worker as well and wasn't slacking off in my work.

When we got back to the job site, I started removing siding, and the cabinet guy pulled up again. He had two other workers with him. I thought, *Lord, please don't speak to me about these guys.* But sure enough, when they walked by, I got a word of knowledge for someone's back. So I started planning how I would share with him and was waiting for an open window without making their boss mad again. Suddenly, this guy who I got a word of knowledge for came out of the house and headed toward the box truck. I followed him and asked if he was having back issues. He said yes. I climbed in the truck, and when I took his hands to start praying for him, his boss came around the corner and started yelling at me again. "You can't be doing that. This is my employee, and he is on the clock."

Something rose up inside me. I replied, with passion and faith, "God is going to heal him. I understand that he is working and will honor that, but at lunch time, on break, I'm going to pray for him." I climbed out of the truck and went back to work. Until lunch, you could cut the tension with a knife. But I had taken a stand and was not going to back down. God had spoken, and I was going to obey him and not be fearful of man.

At lunch, I was sitting in the kitchen with Dan eating lunch, and the guy that I got the word for came around the corner and asked me to please pray for him. So Dan and I together prayed, and afterward, his back felt significantly better. He was very thankful for our prayers.

After lunch, I was working in the kitchen with Dan, and the cabinet crew was working around the corner in the living room. About thirty minutes later, the other employee stuck his head around the corner and whispered, "Are you a Christian? Because I am as well."

I replied quite loudly, "Yeah, I'm a Christian, and we don't have to whisper about it." I was not going to allow anybody to shut me down. I was learning to be bold and unmovable.

The Holy Spirit used the years of working construction with Dan as my evangelism training. I could share hundreds of stories from this time. It was an incredible season of growth, and to this day, as I travel and equip people to share their faith, I base much of teaching on this eight years of time with God and Dan. Not everybody will stand on a crusade field in Pakistan and preach to over 40,000 people or stand in a mosque in Iraq and preach the gospel, but every believer will be at Home Depot, Starbucks, or a gas station and should be equipped to share with others.

God specifically called me to work in construction in this season. He used this time to develop me in hearing his voice and obeying. So if you're reading this and you feel a call to full-time ministry, get a job and work hard unto the Lord while being a light to those around you. When it's time, he will call you into full-time ministry. Many people want to go to the nations and serve the Lord, but they don't share with anybody when they go to Walmart. Start at Walmart and God will open the nations to you.

I hope that my story and testimonies have inspired you and that you are ready to start being used by God everywhere you go. My focus will now shift to equipping you to do exactly this. As we move into the next chapter, I want to be clear that as an evangelist, it's my job to equip the church—you!—to do the work of evangelism. You may not be an evangelist, but you are called to evangelize, which simply means to share your faith with others. "And he gave the apostles, the prophets, the *evangelists*, the shepherds and teachers, to equip the saints for the work of ministry, for building up the body of Christ" (Ephesians 4:11–12, emphasis added).

Jesus gave gifts to the church to equip us for the work of ministry. The evangelist gift is to help activate you in sharing your faith with friends, family, coworkers, and people that you see throughout your day. The job of the evangelist is to help you step out and be bold in your faith so many come to know Jesus. Many have been brought up in churches that look to the pastor as if he does everything. But that's not the way that it was designed to be. God gave gifts to equip the church so that all believers could be used by God to change the world. And how do we change the world? We simply change the world around us.

Keep in mind one last thing before we move into the next chapter. As believers, we don't just do witnessing; we are witnesses. "But you will receive power when the Holy Spirit has come upon you, and you will be my witnesses in Jerusalem and in all Judea and Samaria, and to the end of the earth" (Acts 1:8). A witness simply shares what they witnessed happening. If you are a witness to a car accident, you go to court and tell the judge what you saw. So being a witness for Jesus is simply telling the world what you witnessed Jesus doing for you. It's really that simple. When you walk up to somebody and say "Jesus set me free," you are witnessing.

As a Christian, you are a witness to those around you, no matter what you think. Your life is a witness, and people are watching. My question for you is what are you showing people who are watching your life?

Let's get started being the kind of witnesses that God has called us to be.

6

ARE YOU THINKING WHAT THE FATHER IS THINKING?

I'm a father of four amazing children: Elizabeth (Ellie), Abigale (Abby), Noah, and Esther (Este Besty Boo-Boo Baby). They are truly the joy of my life. In our family, we do daddy dates where I take them out to lunch and buy them a toy. They love to do this although I have not fully figured out if it's because of the ice cream and toys or spending time with dad. Honestly, I don't care. I love spending time with them.

While our family was living in Woodland, Washington, it was time for me to take Ellie out on a daddy-daughter date. She was five years old and loved to go to Subway. I don't know why, but she had it once and was hooked ever since. I'm still trying to figure out how you leave Subway smelling like the restaurant for the next week. Anyway, we decided to go to the Subway at the Walmart in town so we could easily get a toy afterward. After we ordered, we sat down to eat, and Ellie looked at me. "Daddy, are you thinking what I'm thinking?"

Honestly, I 100 percent thought that she was thinking about my wallet and the toy that she was about to buy. But I thought I would play along.

So I said, "No, honey, what are you thinking about?"

Without hesitation, she said, "I'm thinking that we should tell every person in this place about Jesus."

I almost fell out of my chair. We finished our food and shared with everybody that we saw on the way to the toy section and then with the cashier. One guy got really upset at us and started telling us to be quiet, and Ellie stood confidently by my side, not moved by the man because it was her idea to tell everybody about Jesus. I left Walmart in awe at what God had just done through my five-year-old girl.

After this, the Lord began to speak to me and show me truth that has marked my life from that date with Ellie forward. I started wondering why Ellie had the awareness that she had that day about people needing to know about Jesus. She was so quick to hear and obey the Lord and was sensitive to what the Holy Spirit was saying to her. The Lord spoke to me. "She was thinking like her father." When he said this, though, I knew that he was saying that she was thinking like me, her natural father. But why did she think the way that she did that day? What was making her think like her father? At five years old, she was too young to grasp many of the concepts of my sermons. So she didn't think like me because she listened and applied my messages to her life. She never read a book about me because no books were written about me and she couldn't even read. What made her step out and be a witness? What made her think like her daddy?

Well, she spent time with me and grew up around me. Not a day when by that we didn't stop and share about Jesus with others when Ellie was with me in public. Whether at a gas station, grocery store, or the park, I was sharing with people while Ellie was at my side. She was simply thinking and acting like her father that day.

Then the Lord spoke so loudly to me in my spirit. "Can you please get the church thinking like their heavenly Father is thinking?"

This statement from the Lord made was an answer to a prayer that I had been praying for a few weeks prior to this. The Lord had asked me to do an event at Horseshoe Lake Park called

Hope in the Park with The Promise Church. We were going to invite the city to come out and have fun with bounce houses, food and prize giveaways and to hear the gospel. I was asking the Lord how to best mobilize, motivate, and excite the church to be involved in it. I was praying about a message that I was going to share a couple of weeks before the event. I wanted the message to impact the church and motivate them to serve at the event. Little did I know that the Lord would answer my prayer by speaking to me through my daughter. What I learned that day was that the most effective way to get others involved in outreach and sharing their faith is to get them thinking like their Father in heaven.

What is the heavenly Father thinking about? Well, that's easy. Scripture clearly says in John 5:19, "So Jesus explained, "I tell you the truth, the Son can do nothing by himself. He does only what he sees the Father doing. Whatever the Father does, the Son also does" (NLT). So Jesus only did what he saw the Father doing. Luke 19:10 reveals what Jesus came to do. "For the Son of Man came to seek and save those who are lost" (NLT). So what is the Father thinking about? He is thinking about his lost sons and daughters coming home to be with him.

Let me ask you a question: Are you thinking like your heavenly Father? Are you thinking about seeking and saving the lost? If not, I hope that this book will help you to begin to think about what your heavenly Father thinks about. I hope that this book helps you connect with God so that you can begin to do what is on his heart to do in cities and nations all over the world. If a five-year-old can hear and obey, then you can as well.

As I have thought about this story over the years, I have realized an amazing truth about evangelism. That day, I took Ellie out on a date. I was simply loving her by taking her to lunch and buying her a toy. When she was sitting there with me at lunch, her five-year-old mind was working hard, thinking, *How can I love my dad back who is loving me? Well, Dad loves Jesus and loves telling people about Jesus, so I will suggest we do what he likes to do.* Could it be that simple? Think about it for a moment: Could stepping out and sharing your faith with others simply be a way to love God back?

So an important question is, are you spending time with your father? Because if you are spending time with him, then some part of your life will be actively reaching out to others around you and talking to them about Jesus. In this chapter, let's talk about how you can practically spend time with Jesus so you can get to know him and begin to think and do what he does. But first, I have another Ellie story to inspire you to connect with God.

About a year after the event at Subway, Ellie and I planned another date. She wanted to go to Chuck-E-Cheese. Honestly, Chuck's Cheese, as I call it, is one of my least favorite places to go. It's like taking a few twenty-dollar bills and lighting them on fire while being surrounded by overly stimulated kids for a few tickets that get you a Tootsie Roll and a plastic ring while eating pizza that tastes like cardboard covered with fake cheese.

But since Ellie wanted to go, we went. My plan was to get in and out as quickly as possible while spending as little as money as possible. It was Saturday, and the place was, of course, packed with people, overloading the senses. We went in, won some tickets, and got out in a maximum of about twenty minutes. On the way out, Ellie was holding my hand. She stopped and looked at me. "Daddy, we didn't tell anybody about Jesus in there." My eyes got big because she was right, but even more than that, my six-year-old had become my evangelism accountability partner. We turned around and immediately began to share with people. Again, why did she think this way? Because she was around her daddy, who thinks about seeking and saving the lost.

The Secret Place

"But you, when you pray, go into your room, and when you have shut your door, pray to your Father who is in the secret place; and your Father who sees in secret will reward you openly" (Matthew 6:6 NKJV).

This Scripture is one of my all-time favorites. First, it says *when* you pray, not *if* you pray. As believers, we pray and connect with God. We must understand that connecting with God is not the same for everybody. Some need to be alone, locked behind closed doors, and others need to be in nature on a walk. Still others connect with God through many different ways. There is no exact formula for how to connect with God; it's deeply personal for each and every person. What is important is that you connect with God daily. At Mercy Culture, our vision statement is to take people from corporate encounters with God to daily personal encounters with God. If people can connect with God daily, it changes everything. One of the sayings at our church is that hard things become easy in the presence of God. What is hard outside of the presence of God becomes easy when you do it with him. So evangelism becomes easy when you connect with God daily.

Another highlight in this verse is when you meet with your Father in secret, he will reward you openly. It is absolutely wonderful that the father wants to give you an open reward. What is that reward? It's more of his presence and the ability to hear his voice in your daily life. I like to think about it this way. If you meet with him in the morning and hear his voice, you can hear his voice clearly at lunch while standing in line waiting to order or at your job site working with other carpenters that need an encounter with God. If you connect with God in secret, you can hear his voice in public much more clearly.

We are often too busy and distracted to slow down and connect with God. We wake up and instantly get on our phones, look at our calendars, and start the rat race for the day. Yes, we are all busy and running from one activity to the next, but when we connect with God, all that we are doing becomes that much easier. Even if we only connect with him for a short time, that's not important. He is outside of time, so the length of time doesn't matter but the connection. It is so important to connect with God daily. Remove the religious lies that say it needs to look like your pastor or friend who sit with God for three hours a day. Don't play the comparison game and or fall into a trap that says it needs to be a certain length of time. Just make time to get real with God and connect with him.

This Scripture in John 6 will help this come to life. Jesus feeds the five thousand. Let's pick up in the story in John 6:10–13.

Jesus said, "Have the people sit down" Now there was much grass in the place. So the men sat down, about five thousand in number. Jesus then took the loaves, and when he had given thanks, he distributed them to those who were seated. So also the fish, as much as they wanted. And when they had eaten their fill, he told his disciples, "Gather up the leftover fragments, that nothing may be lost." So they gathered them up and filled twelve baskets with fragments from the five barley loaves left by those who had eaten.

I want to point out here that Jesus had them sit down before he fed them. Maybe some were in the crowd that never sat down. Maybe they were skeptical and thought that they would just stand off to the side and see what this guy named Jesus would do. The passage said, though, that those that sat down, he fed. My question is, do you sit with the Lord daily? Because unless you sit with the Lord, you won't be fed. Again, I'm not saying that you need to get in your actual closet, shut the door, and sit down. You can sit with the Lord on a prayer walk or driving to work. It is about connection more than about how you connect. So do you sit with him daily? Are you connecting with your Father? Are you eating daily bread from heaven? If not, it's time to start today.

Imagine that my friend Alonzo comes to my home for dinner, and Chelsea had spent all day preparing a wonderful meal for him. When Alonzo enters the house he just takes off his shoes and starts walking all over and doesn't stop while he is at my house. I give him a drink, but I keep asking him to sit down so that we can give him the meal that we prepared for him. But as hard as we try, he doesn't sit down the entire time that he is at our house. He just walks in circles from one room to the next.

We finally give up and sit down and eat without him. His plate is sitting there full but getting cold. All he had to do was sit down and enjoy a beautifully prepared meal, but instead, he missed the opportunity to eat. I know that this is a funny story, but it really applies to many in the church today. God wants us to sit with him and enjoy a beautiful meal that he has made for us, but we don't slow down long enough to eat with him. If we don't slow down to be with him, we won't think like him throughout the day.

The Scripture said that those who sat down with him "ate as much they wanted". The Lord wants to satisfy us and meet all of our needs in his presence. Psalm 16:11 says, "You make known to me the path of life; in your presence there is fullness of joy; at your right hand are pleasures forevermore." God wants to bless us as we sit with him; he wants to fill us up until nothing is lacking in our lives. Matthew 6:33 says, "But seek first the kingdom of God and his righteousness, and all these things will be added to you." That's right, if we seek first his kingdom, then all the things that we need will be added to us. How do we seek first his kingdom? We first start by spending time with him.

Not only did they eat all that they wanted but the Scripture tells us that they also had twelve baskets of leftovers, one for each of the disciples. What is the meaning of twelve baskets of leftovers? I think the Lord was showing them that if they sit and are filled by His Word, the bread, then they will be fully satisfied and have leftovers to give away to others.

So often, Christians can be so selfish and needy. They have not been filled by the Word of God, the bread of God. Jesus said in Matthew 4:4, "But he answered, 'It is written, "Man shall not live by bread alone, but by every word that comes from the mouth of God."'" We have to connect with God so that we can live. Jesus tells us right after the feeding of the five thousand in John 6:33 that he is the bread of life. "For the bread of God is he who comes down from heaven and gives life to the world." We need to connect with God daily so that we can have our daily bread. When Jesus teaches his disciples to pray, he says to pray this way. "Give us this day our daily bread" (Matthew 6:11).

If we don't eat our daily bread, we walk around hungry and end up taking from others instead of walking around full and having a basket of leftovers to share with others. It's amazing when you meet with God and leave that encounter full and then go and give people Jesus from the overflow of your time with God. We are meant to live out of our relationship with God.

Today, as I was writing this chapter in Granbury, Texas, God spoke to me out of the overflow of my relationship with him. On my way out of the cafe where I was writing, I got a word of knowledge for the owners of the restaurant. I walked over to them. "Hey, so sorry to bug you but God speaks to me often about people. I felt that he spoke to me and told me that I needed to pray for one of your shoulders."

Shocked, the wife pointed to her husband and said that would be for him. I then asked, "Is your left shoulder worse than your right shoulder?" And he responded that it was. They were both believers but were amazed that God would speak to me about them in such a personal way.

The wife said, "Wow, this is crazy that you could come in here and know that about us even though you've never seen us before." After I prayed, we said our goodbyes. You'd better believe they were moved by that encounter. Why did that happen? Because

I sit down with Jesus daily, I think about what he thinks about. Because I spent time with him in the morning, I could hear his voice more clearly at the cafe. If you begin to sit with the Lord, you too could be used in this same way. God is looking to partner with you in doing things just like this every day.

Another day, our family was at Taco Bell in Woodland. Please don't judge me. Taco Bell food is delicious at least once a year, if not twice. The new Taco Bell in Woodland was a big deal for our little town, so the entire restaurant was full with not a seat open in the whole place. To give you some context, when Walmart opened in our town, a few years prior, people slept outside to be the first inside when it officially opened. Walking through Walmart for the first time, I thought, *This is crazy. I can't believe we have a Walmart.* If you come from a small town, I'm sure you can relate.

Okay, back to Taco Bell. My family was sitting there, eating our food, when I noticed a guy across the restaurant, sitting at his table eating. I felt like sharing the gospel with him, but I didn't know if he was ready to receive or not. So I kept eating and asking myself if he was ready to hear the gospel. All of a sudden Ellie, who was five years old at the time, looked at me and asked, "Daddy, do you think that I should go share the gospel with that man?" I asked what man, and she pointed to the same man that I was looking at. The restaurant was packed, and this man was in the corner. Ellie had no idea that I was looking at him or thinking about sharing with him.

I was so taken aback at her question that I looked at her. "You should ask God and do what he says to do."

Ellie closed her eyes and bowed her head and then quickly opened them. "He said go!"

At that, Chelsea looked at me. "If he told her to go, he told you to go." God had set me up and was teaching me a very important lesson, and he was using my five-year-old as the teacher.

Ellie and I stood and began to walk toward the man through the crowded restaurant as she led me across the restaurant. I was following my five-year-old's obedience. Talk about humbling! When we reached him, she said, "Jesus loves you." That was what she knew to say. She then looked at me to do the rest.

The moment that Ellie said that, the Holy Spirit gave me a word of knowledge for the man's right knee. I then said, "My name is Chris, and my daughter felt led to come and tell you about Jesus. I was wondering if you were having trouble with your right knee. Oftentimes, God speaks to us about people because he wants you to know that he loves you." The man was very interested in what we were saying and began to tell us that he did have a bad right knee and that he would let us pray for him. So right there, we prayed for him and believed God for healing. When we were done praying, we asked him if he felt any better, and he said that he wouldn't know until later that day. He said that it hurt when he ran and that he was going for a run later and that he would take our number and let us know. I shared the simple gospel with him, but he really wasn't open to it, so we went back over to our table, finished eating, and headed home.

Later that night, at 10:08 p.m., the man texted me. What the heck did you do to me? I went for a six-mile run, and my knee doesn't hurt at all. He was training for a marathon, and God completely healed his knee.

I quickly texted back. This is Jesus. He doesn't just want to heal your knee, he wants to heal your heart and give you the gift of salvation. He didn't respond.

The next day, I was with my family in Walmart, and when I came around the corner of the frozen-food section, a man was standing at the other end, looking at me with big eyes. It was the same man whose knee was healed. I didn't recognize him for a minute, but we quickly pushed our cart toward him and began a conversation. He was so thankful that his knee was healed, so I began to share the gospel with him again. But he said that he was not ready to fully give his life to Jesus. God was absolutely chasing this man, and seeds of the love of God and the gospel were planted deep in his heart because a five-year-old said yes to Jesus when her father was trying to figure out if he should go and share or not. The harvest is ripe, and the laborers are few. It's time to get to work in the harvest fields.

7

THE ORIGINAL CALL NEVER CHANGED

A few years ago, I was in Iraq with a team of people, working alongside a missionary and his family that have been living in the nation of Iraq since 2014. Part of our ministry was equipping Muslim-background believers (MBB's) to share their faith and then taking them out and activating them on the streets. Sharing your faith in Iraq is a bit different than sharing in America. The stakes are higher and the cost is greater, especially for those who live there and won't be leaving a few days later like I did. After we spent a couple of sessions equipping people, it was time to head out on a street outreach to activate them. I was paired with a man we'll call Ben for his safety.

Here's a little bit of Ben's back story to give you more context. Ben and his wife were both raised as Muslims. One day, Ben's wife had an encounter with Jesus, who told her three things: I'm the Son of God, obey me, and tell others about me. If that wasn't enough, she actually had another similar encounter with Jesus when he repeated the same three things to her. So she became a believer and follower of Jesus. She began to tell her husband about Jesus, so he began to search for God too. They started attending church meetings. Ben was praying one day to God and said, "If you are real, reveal yourself to me."

As he was on his knees while my missionary friend was laying hands on him, the audible voice of God said, "I'm the Son of God. Obey me and tell others about me." So he became a believer and began to follow after Jesus with his wife. I met Ben two years after this encounter, but he had not yet openly shared about Jesus with anyone, so this would be a new experience.

We went out together to start the outreach on the streets. We simply wanted to start conversations with people that were walking out of and into businesses and restaurants. Ben seemed to think I would talk and he would interpret, which is a big step for somebody that is sharing Jesus in the Middle East.

We stopped two people and began sharing with them about Jesus. I didn't seem to be getting anywhere. All of a sudden, the Lord brought a brilliant idea to my mind. Instead of trying to share with these guys, it would make a lot more sense if Ben did. I mean, he was born in the nation of Iraq and was a Muslim at one point and had heard the audible voice of God tell him that Jesus is the Son of God. How much of a better witness can you have?

So I told the two men that Ben was now going to stop translating and share his own testimony. Instead, Ben looked at me. "What are you doing? Are you trying to get me killed?"

I responded, "No, I'm trying to help you obey God. Did you hear God say share with others? If you did, then he is with you." He thought for a moment and then turned back to those two men and started sharing his testimony. As he spoke, you could see that it really impacted them. After this, I couldn't hold him back from sharing. It was like a lion had been released from its cage. I actually see this often; once a person steps out in faith and sees that God is with them, they find great boldness.

You may be reading this and thinking, *Wow, that is a pretty cool story. But Chris, I have never heard the audible voice of God like Ben. So I don't think I need to share like him.* Well, then, if you need to hear the audible voice of God, then read the Bible out loud. He tells you to get out there and share with people who need to know Jesus.

A life that is aware of the Father's heart where you step out and share with others is actually not just for some Christians but for all believers. It is the original call and has never changed. What do I mean by the original call? The original call is what Jesus has called us to do as born-again believers. That is right, we have been called to do something: the Great Commission, not the great suggestion.

Allow this passage of Scripture in Matthew 28:16–20 to define the call.

Now the eleven disciples went to Galilee, to the mountain to which Jesus had directed them. And when they saw him they worshiped him, but some doubted. And Jesus came and said to them, "All authority in heaven and on earth has been given to me. Go therefore and make disciples of all nations, baptizing them in the name of the Father and of the Son and of the Holy Spirit, teaching them to observe all that I have commanded you. And behold, I am with you always, to the end of the age."

Jesus has called us to make disciples of all nations. That seems like a huge task, but if every believer began to do their part it's more than possible to do this and win the nations to Jesus. The Christian call is bigger than just trying to get your family to church on a Sunday morning. Trust me, I know that can be difficult as Chelsea and I have four kids and sometimes just getting to church on time without any meltdowns is a miracle. But we are called to so much more than just attending church and cheer from the sidelines as our pastors and favorite ministers further the kingdom of God. We are called to be part of something so much bigger and more exciting.

For the rest of this chapter, let's look at three things that will really help us identify the original call and if we are willing to count the cost and to participate in that call.

The Call

When Jesus walked the earth two thousand years ago, he called people to follow him. Matthew 4:18–20 tells us about one of those occasions. "While walking by the Sea of Galilee, he saw two brothers, Simon (who is called Peter) and Andrew his brother, casting a net into the sea, for they were fishermen. And he said to them, 'Follow me, and I will make you fishers of men.' Immediately they left their nets and followed him."

When Jesus said this, he didn't have them follow him into a classroom to do a Bible study. They began to follow him as he went out to do what he came to earth to do: seek and save the lost (Luke 19:10) and proclaim liberty to the captives. Let's look at Luke 4:18–19. "The Spirit of the Lord is upon me, because he has anointed me to proclaim good news to the poor. He has sent me to proclaim liberty to the captives and recovering of sight to the blind, to set at liberty those who are oppressed, to proclaim the year of the Lord's favor."

Jesus came to be a fisher of men and to equip his followers to be fishers of men as well. The twelve disciples and other followers of Jesus who called him Rabbi knew that they were called to do the same things he did. This is why Jesus said, "Follow me" and began to heal the sick, cast out demons, and raise the dead. He was showing them and us what they were called to do as well. Yes, it's hard to believe we can do what Jesus did but look at these verses and see that Jesus wants to use your life to reach others.

"And these signs will accompany those who believe: in my name they will cast out demons; they will speak in new tongues; they will pick up serpents with their hands; and if they drink any deadly poison, it will not hurt them; they will lay their hands on the sick, and they will recover" (Mark 16:17–18).

"Truly, truly, I say to you, whoever believes in me will also do the works that I do; and greater works than these will he do, because I am going to the Father. Whatever you ask in my name, this I will do, that the Father may be glorified in the Son. If you ask me anything in my name, I will do it" (John 14:12–14).

When I read these verses, I think, *Okay, that is amazing. But what is the purpose of these signs accompanying believers and believers doing greater works?* It's so that more people would come to know Jesus. Greater works isn't that we will do more impressive things than Jesus, like walk on water longer or multiply more food; it's that more Christians will be doing his work all over the world. A greater number of works will be taking place. And what's so cool is that you and I can be a part of the greater works spoken of in these verses if we say yes to the original call that has not changed.

The Commission

When Jesus called his disciples to follow him, he said, "I will make you fishers of men," which we just talked about in the last section. But what did Jesus say to his disciples as he was about to be taken up to heaven? "Go therefore and make disciples of all nations, baptizing them in the name of the Father and of the Son and of the Holy Spirit" (Matthew 28:19). Remember, this is the Great Commission, not the great suggestion. The Great Commission was to go and make disciples. This was the job description that he left us to accomplish as the church.

Can you imagine being there that day with Jesus as he made this final statement? I don't know about you, but I would be saying, "Jesus, are you sure this is a good idea? You just died, rose again from the dead, and spent forty days meeting with us and telling us about the kingdom of God. Not to mention, you have been showing up by walking through walls, which has been freaking us out a bit. And Thomas is having a hard time believing all of this, and honestly, so am I. Is this the best plan you can think of? Wouldn't it be better if you stayed and we followed you around and watched you do all the stuff like we have for the last three and a half years?"

Can you imagine Jesus ascending into heaven as I and a few others grabbed a hold of his ankles, trying to keep him on earth? Think about it for a moment. This doesn't seem like the best business plan, does it? He was leaving the expansion of the kingdom and its mission to make disciples to a group of people who just had their faith tested. Some of them, like Peter, failed that test and denied Jesus. Even though Jesus restored him, wouldn't it make more sense for Jesus to wait a little longer to see if Peter and the boys could be trusted? But that's not what happened because Jesus's plan is way better than any plan that we can come up with, no matter how great we think our ideas are. "Nevertheless, I tell you the truth: it is to your advantage that I go away, for if I do not go away, the Helper will not come to you. But if I go, I will send him to you" (John 16:7).

If Jesus would not have gone away to be with the Father, he would not have sent the Holy Spirit and that would have been big trouble for the Great Commission. But he did go away and did send the Holy Spirit to empower us. I often say, "Christ in you is better than Christ beside you." Think about it. Jesus even said that it was better that he go away so that he could send the Holy Spirit to empower us to fulfill the call to fish for men and the Great Commission to make disciples.

Remember that you are not called to do this in your own strength or power but by the empowerment of the Holy Spirit. Read these Scriptures. He is the Lord of the harvest and empowers us to do what he calls us to do.

"And said to them, "Thus it is written, that the Christ should suffer and on the third day rise from the dead, and that repentance for the forgiveness of sins should be proclaimed in his name to all nations, beginning from Jerusalem. You are witnesses of these things. And behold, I am sending the promise of my Father upon you. But stay in the city until you are clothed with power from on high" (Luke 24:46–49).

"But you will receive power when the Holy Spirit has come upon you, and you will be my witnesses in Jerusalem and in all Judea and Samaria, and to the end of the earth" (Acts 1:8).

"So then the Lord Jesus, after he had spoken to them, was taken up into heaven and sat down at the right hand of God. And they went out and preached everywhere, while the Lord worked with them and confirmed the message by accompanying signs" (Mark 16:19–20).

These verses are so encouraging and give so much faith to the reader that God is for us and is there with us as we work with him to fulfill the Great Commission. The next verse is a bridge to the third and final point of this chapter, the cost of following Jesus.

"I have been crucified with Christ. It is no longer I who live, but Christ who lives in me. And the life I now live in the flesh I live by faith in the Son of God, who loved me and gave himself for me" (Galatians 2:20).

What we often focus on in this Scripture is the section that says "it's no longer I who live, but Christ who lives in me." This is such a powerful truth. Another Scripture says it this way. "If the Spirit of him who raised Jesus from the dead dwells in you, he who raised Christ Jesus from the dead will also give life to your mortal bodies through his Spirit who dwells in you" (Romans 8:11). Many people excitedly preach, "The same spirit that raised Christ from the dead is in you. You can change the world with Jesus!" This is true, but we must understand that in order to experience that amazing life-giving power to its fullest, we must be crucified with Christ. "I appeal to you therefore, brothers, by the mercies of God, to present your bodies as a living sacrifice, holy and acceptable to God, which is your spiritual worship" (Romans 12:1). A living sacrifice. Have you ever really thought about that? What does it mean to be a living sacrifice? We'll focus on this in the last section of this chapter: the cost of following Jesus. Again, he wants to empower us but we must count the cost before we receive his power to complete the job he gave us to do.

The Cost

First, let's read the words of Jesus so that you don't think I'm being too extreme. Jesus was quite serious when it came to laying down your life to follow him. I fear that many in the American church have turned following Jesus into coming to church on Sunday morning once a month and trying to be a good person for the rest of the year. The Christian life was never supposed to be about this. Christianity was never meant to be a social club or a self-improvement plan that we apply when we need help. It was meant to be a death-to-life reality that shifts and changes every aspect of the Christian's life. Jesus is not just Savior; he is Lord and Savior. He is actually not your Savior unless he is first your Lord. We were once dead in our trespasses and sins, but we are now alive in Christ. It's death to life! It's black and white.

"Then Jesus told his disciples, "If anyone would come after me, let him deny himself and take up his cross and follow me. For whoever would save his life will lose it, but whoever loses his life for my sake will find it" (Matthew 16:24–25).

"For none of us lives to himself, and none of us dies to himself. For if we live, we live to the Lord, and if we die, we die to the Lord. So then, whether we live or whether we die, we are the Lord's" (Romans 14:7–8).

We must remember that following Jesus means denying yourself, picking up your cross, and following him. My heart for this section is that you see the real cost of following Jesus and that you count that cost fully and say yes to him, no matter what. Many want the power of God to move through their lives and want to be used by God to do great works for his kingdom, but they are not willing to fully count the cost.

Remember the story that I told you about Ben, who lives in Iraq. Would you agree that his costs far outweigh the costs that we face in the West? Sharing our faith with somebody might cost us our reputation, whereas sharing his faith could actually cost him his life. When you put it in that context, it's quite sobering. I don't want to brush over this but really want to ask you to count the cost. To emphasize this idea of counting the cost, Jesus told this parable to a crowd:

> Now great crowds accompanied him, and he turned and said to them, "If anyone comes to me and does not hate his own father and mother and wife and children and brothers and sisters, yes, and even his own life, he cannot be my disciple. Whoever does not bear his own cross and come after me cannot be my disciple. For which of you, desiring to build a tower, does not first sit down and count the cost, whether he has enough to complete it? Otherwise, when he has laid a foundation and is not able to finish, all who see it begin to mock him, saying, 'This man began to build and was not able to finish.' Or what king, going out to encounter another king in war, will not sit down first and deliberate whether he is able with ten thousand to meet him who comes against him with twenty thousand? And if not, while the other is yet a great way off, he sends a delegation and asks for terms of peace. So therefore, any one of you who does not renounce all that he has cannot be my disciple. (Luke 14 :25–33)

Would you be willing to give your life for Jesus? Would you be willing to stand for him in extreme circumstances and persecution? By the grace of God, any believer who has counted the cost could do it. When you read these words, did different fears rise in your heart? That's okay, that is needed. Take those fears to God and ask him to remove them, count the cost, and go all in with Jesus. There is no better time than now.

In the West, when we read passages of Scripture like the ones listed below, we don't really connect to them fully because persecution is not happening here, especially not in America at the moment. But read them as if you are Ben and ask yourself if you're ready to count the cost and go all in. True fire falls only on all-in sacrifice and obedience to the lordship of Jesus Christ.

"What I tell you in the dark, say in the light, and what you hear whispered, proclaim on the housetops. And do not fear those who kill the body but cannot kill the soul. Rather fear him who can destroy both soul and body in hell" (Matthew 10:27–28).

"So everyone who acknowledges me before men, I also will acknowledge before my Father who is in heaven, but whoever denies me before men, I also will deny before my Father who is in heaven" (Matthew 10:32–33).

"Do you think that I have come to give peace on earth? No, I tell you, but rather division. For from now on in one house there will be five divided, three against two and two against three. They will be divided, father against son and son against father, mother against daughter and daughter against mother, mother-in-law against her daughter-in-law and daughter-in-law against mother-in-law" (Luke 12:51–53).

On one trip to Iraq, we had the honor of sitting with a pastor who has given his life to the people of his nation. Many Christians in Iraq, when they get saved, try to leave the country due to the persecution that follows. Many times, this pastor has been asked, "Why don't you leave?" His answer has been and will continue to be "because I'm called to these people, and I am going to sow my life into this land." He then told us with love in his eyes to find a place to sow our lives into.

We asked him what he thought the biggest difference was between American and Iraqi Christians. His response was "what you call sanctification." We asked him to explain. He said, "Well, in America, people make a casual commitment to Jesus and then in the following months and years decide if they are really serious when they face different troubles and challenges. Think about it. We might say, "Well, next week I will commit to that, or at the beginning of the year, I'm going to focus and get right with God." Due to the lack of persecution that we face, we can have a very casual response to the words of Jesus. In Iraq, a person might take six months or a year to say yes to Jesus. They truly have to count the cost. They have to be willing to lose family, friends, their job, and income over this decision. It takes them time to count the cost, but once they do, they go all in and say yes, truly denying themselves. Persecution produces an environment that causes a believer to count the cost more fully.

I'm going to ask you a series of questions that are designed to make you think about the cost. Don't get overwhelmed by these questions. Just honestly ask yourself if you have counted the cost and understand we are all growing to be more like Jesus. None of us have arrived yet. Do any of the following make you uncomfortable?

- sharing your faith with the attendant at the gas station
- taking your Bible to work and reading it on your lunch break in public
- going to a family gathering and sharing that you have a relationship with Jesus
- wearing a shirt that boldly proclaims Jesus or the gospel
- not listing your pronouns at work
- refusing to wear a LGBTQI+ sports jersey for your team pride night
- being a Christian with conservative views on your college campus
- not laughing and participating in dirty jokes at work
- walking out of a movie that doesn't honor God at the theater when all your friends are there

I could go on and on with examples of things to make you slow down and ask yourself whether you have really counted the cost or are you in a place where you are living more than Christ is living in you? I can't say this enough: Count the cost and die to yourself because on the other side of your surrender is an amazing Spirit empowered life that will change those around you. Don't allow fear to hold you back, say yes to Jesus.

Let's look at Matthew 16:24–25 again. "Then Jesus told his disciples, "If anyone would come after me, let him deny himself and take up his cross and follow me. For whoever would save his life will lose it, but whoever loses his life for my sake will find it."

Remember that Jesus is God. He says that if we "try to hold on to our life we will lose it, but if we lose it for his sake we will find it." This is a process, one I have been on ever since encountering God when I was eighteen years old. You are in process as well. God is not looking for perfection; he is looking for obedience and growth. We all start somewhere, and I celebrate where you are at in your journey as I am lovingly encouraging you forward into more.

A few years ago, I was leading an outreach at a school where I was working. The main focus was evangelism. People came from around the US and world to be trained to go out and share their faith. These students all had a heart to share but were in different stages of growing in confidence. One of the ladies was in her fifties and was so willing to share but struggled with fear on the actual outreaches. After each outreach, we would come back together and share testimonies of what God had done. She shared such a beautiful testimony that really has helped me equip others ever since then.

She was on an outreach and ended up at a restaurant. She saw a woman that she knew she was supposed to share with. When she thought about going over to share, she started crying and shaking in great fear. But despite the fear and in obedience, with tears still in her eyes, she walked right up to the woman. The woman asked her, "Are you okay?"

She responded, "Yes, I want to share Jesus with you, but I'm really scared."

The woman then replied, "Well, I'm an atheist, but please share with me." So she shared her testimony and the simple gospel. At that moment, she didn't win the lady to the Lord but sowed amazing gospel seed, overcame fear, and was obedient to the Holy Spirit.

If a five-year-old can do it, you can too. If a scared and crying woman in her fifties can do it, you can too. Just step out in faith and go for it.

8

GO, GROW, TRULY KNOW

I will never forget my thirty-first birthday. Chelsea woke me up and excitedly hurried me down the hall into the kitchen where a present was on the table. I thought, *Where are the kids*? It was early, and Ellie and Abby were already gone. Chelsea was fully dressed, which was unusual after we had kids. I was almost always awake before her. She enthusiastically handed me the present, which was super light. I don't know about you, but I don't like light presents. I like heavy ones with some weight to them. So I opened it and found a folded piece of paper. I looked at Chelsea, and she took it out of my hands, unfolded it, and handed it back to me. I read it: Congratulations! You are going skydiving today." Before I even had time to process the fact that I was going skydiving that very day—not next week but that day!—Chelsea immediately said, "Hurry up and get dressed. We need to leave right now, and the car is already running." We lived above her parents' garage in a loft, and the car was running below.

When we got in the car, Chelsea looked at me. "Are you excited?"

In the moment, I manned up. "Yes." But honestly, inside, I was still processing that I was a few hours away from jumping out of an airplane.

She said, "You always told me that you wanted to go skydiving, so I wanted to make that happen." To make matters even more scary, nobody that I knew was going with me, and Chelsea couldn't because she was pregnant with Noah. I had always shared very confidently around family and friends that I wanted to go skydiving, so Chelsea just figured I was ready.

The truth was that I would have liked to go skydiving, on my terms, when I was ready. I would have liked to plan a trip a month out so that I could mentally prepare myself for what I was about to do. The truth, though, is that I would probably still to this day not have gone skydiving.

Many people are the same way with evangelism. They say they want to share their faith, but they want to do it when they're ready on their terms. And they never find themselves ready, so they go year after year without sharing their faith with others.

Two different kinds of people are reading this book: those who have skydived and those who have not. If you have skydived, you will fully relate with what I'm about to share. If you have not gone skydiving, then follow along as I explain this experience. To clarify, being in a wind-tunnel skydiving simulator may be cool, but that is not the same as jumping out of a plane at eighteen thousand feet. A simulator is like going to missions school but never actually going out on the mission field. Until you go, you will never really know. You could actually have read many books and textbooks and watched many YouTube videos, gathering a lot of intellectual knowledge. But I have more experience than you do because I have done it and you haven't. The same principle applies when it comes to evangelism. They have read the books and textbooks, listened to the messages, and have evangelism theory down pat, but they have never shared the gospel with anybody. The world doesn't need a theory but an encounter with God.

I asked Chelsea where we were going and she said that she found a place in Portland, about an hour and fifteen minutes away. It was a long drive. I don't know if Chelsea could tell, but I was nervous and trying to find a way out of it. But again, I was a man and had said many times that I wanted to do this, so on the outside, I was trying to keep cool.

When we pulled onto the compound with the planes, my stomach dropped but it was too late. We were there, and I was going to jump. I walked into the office with Chelsea. They greeted us, asked us to take a seat, and told us that they would be right with us. A big group of people was about to jump, but I couldn't go with them because it was full. So I had to wait a bit longer. The group left, and I was the only one still there.

About five minutes later, a guy came over to me. "Hey, instead of waiting for the next group, why don't you go with us? We are going in about fifteen minutes." They just happened to be a group of professional skydivers that jumped about ten times a day. I agreed. "Great! Just go watch the movie, and then we will leave." He didn't know that the movie was already halfway over. I walked in just as the video was explaining that skydiving was dangerous. You do it at your own risk, and you will need to sign a waiver. They came and got me before the movie ended. I think they needed to document that I had seen the movie for liability purposes. I signed the waiver, and the guy that I was jumping with said, "Okay, it's time to jump."

He then mentioned that they normally spent more time explaining the jump and training, but since it was just me, he would show me a few pointers quickly, and we would go. I was jumping tandem with him, so he showed me how we would be connected together. Then we headed toward the plane. When we got outside the office, a group of about ten professional skydivers were waiting for us. They all were telling me how much I would love it. I smiled to hide my concern. I wasn't going out with ten rookies but ten uber-experienced people.

The plane took off, and when the door shut and the wheels came off the ground, I decided to share my testimony with all of them. So I started sharing, and they listened. The pilot then said we were at eighteen hundred feet. I thought, *Okay, it's time to jump*. But nobody was moving.

Then I realized that we weren't jumping at eighteen hundred feet, so I calmly asked the guy I was with what height we were jumping at. "Eighteen thousand feet." My stomach rolled.

The plane kept climbing, and after I shared my testimony with all of them, they asked me how I was feeling and if I was afraid. "No, I don't fear death. I'm going to be with Jesus when I die." That was more of a statement of faith than a reality at that moment.

When we got close to eighteen thousand feet, my skydiving partner told me we were close and strapped us together tightly. I asked him if somebody who he went with had ever refused to jump at the last minute. (I was thinking about not jumping.) He said he had never not jumped. Suddenly, they opened the back sliding door, and we slid down the bench together and moved to the door so that our feet were hanging out. All the pros waited for us to go first. They were hanging out the door, watching me. They had told me that because it was just me that we were going to fall together in a circle holding hands and that it would be awesome. Right before we jumped, he told me, "You won't think that you can breathe, but you can. Just take deep breaths." I thought he would count to three, but he counted to one, grabbed my head, and pulled it back. We rolled out of the plane.

For the first few seconds, I didn't breathe. This is like many people on their first outreach. Then I remembered that he told me that I could breathe, so I began to think over and over, *I can breathe, I can breathe,* and started taking deep breaths. If he hadn't told me that I could breathe, I might have passed out. As we fell, I closed my eyes and gripped my chest strap. Then, somebody tried to grab my arm. I opened my eyes at a circle of people around me, looking at me and smiling. They pried my hands free, and we were free falling in a circle. I started to breathe more easily, and for a few moments that felt like an hour, we fell together. One at a time, they waved goodbye and flew off in different directions. It was so cool! Before you knew it, we pulled our parachute and slowly descended to the landing zone. What an unforgettable experience! They asked if I wanted a video. "No, I will never forget that." Close to five years later, I still remember every second.

I shared this story because so often, in our Christian walks, all we have is a theory, and we never actually step out and do it to see if that theory works. I have talked to many people who have theories on evangelism, and they critique the way I do it. I have asked these people in love how many people they have seen won to the Lord with their theories. Most of the time, they haven't won anybody to the Lord. The world needs people who will believe God and go for it. Will you be one? Will you go so that you can grow, so that you can truly know God and his power?

You don't need to be a great evangelist to share your faith. You just need to realize that the great Evangelist is with you. Just like when I jumped out of the plane that day, I didn't need to fear anything. A trained professional was on my back. I the same way, you don't need to fear anything because God is with you. You just need to have faith and jump.

Take a moment and think about the people in your life that you look up to when it comes to their walk with the Lord: maybe a grandparent, a pastor from your church, or somebody that you have not met but read about that was used mightily for God. For example, Reinhard Bonnke, Rees Howells, D.L. Moody, Praying John Hyde, Billy Graham, Heidi Baker, Dr. Michael Brown, Bill Johnson, and many more have been an inspiration to my faith. What do all these great men and women of God have in common? They all decided to activate their faith. They are a source of inspiration to so many because at some point, they decided to say yes to God and go for it in faith. All these men and women that have gone for it in faith are showing us what is possible for us. But we must step out of our comfort zone and go for it.

'How does this man know letters, having never studied?' Jesus answered them and said, 'My doctrine is not mine, but his who sent me. If anyone wills to do his will, he shall know concerning the doctrine, whether it is from God or whether I speak on my own authority'" (John 7:14–17 NKJV).

The Scripture says, "if any wills to do his will." Do you see that? It says "do his will," not just study his will or talk about his will or even memorize his will. Again, let this sink in. "Do his will." We can know a lot of information about God and his Word but actually never step out and put it into practice. If we don't step out in faith and take action with what we know, even if what we know is right and true, we will never see the fruit of that truth. Many Christians live this way because they know a lot of theories about the Bible but don't experience that truth because they never step out in faith.

This book's focus is evangelism, and we will keep to that theme. But for a moment, I want to show you that this truth does not just apply to sharing your faith with others but actually to every aspect of your Christian life. Nothing in your Christian life was meant to be just a theory or a song that you sing on Sunday morning. Everything that we read about in the Bible is meant to be walked out in the Christian life and fought for in our daily reality. Let's look at a few examples.

Giving

"But when you do a charitable deed, do not let your left hand know what your right hand is doing, that your charitable deed may be in secret; and your Father who sees in secret will Himself reward you openly" (Matthew 6:3 NKJV). You see the language again is "when you do your charitable deed." The ESV says, "When you give." As Christians, we are supposed to give but many never give.

Let's say that you listened to all the messages on biblical giving that you could find on YouTube and read all the books that talked about giving on Amazon in one year. At the end of the year, your heart was burning to give and see God move through your finances. You excitedly start telling everybody all the truths and principles that you have learned about giving during the year, but the entire year, you never give, not even a dollar, to a charity. I'm sorry to say, but all you have is a theory on giving; even if your theory is right, you won't experience the joy and benefits of giving unless you give. At a certain point, you have to give. The Scripture says, "And your father, who sees in secret, will himself reward you openly." This means if you don't give, you will not receive the reward of giving that the Father wants to give you because you never did the will of God. I want to give so that I can be rewarded by my Father.

This story demonstrates the power of giving and the open rewards that come with it. We must understand that we don't give to get but that we give out of obedience to the Lord. The truth is that when we live in obedience to God and do what his Word commands us to do, we will experience the blessings of God and be given what we need when we need it to fulfill what he has called us to fulfill on earth. Matthew 6:33 says, "Seek the kingdom of God above all else, and live righteously, and he will give you everything you need" (NLT). If you live a life of obedience to God, you will have what you need when you need it, not what you want when you want it.

In 2018, when Chelsea and I moved to Texas the first time, we were taking a massive step of faith. I really had just made it to a place in full-time ministry at The Promise Church in Washington where we were making decent money. For the first time in our married life and ministry, we could begin to think about building a house for our family. We had lived from faith to faith and check to check for years. Not one time had God not provided for us, but we had definitely been down to twenty dollars in our bank account on many occasions. Right when we got to a place of being somewhat comfortable financially, the Lord spoke to us about moving to Fort Worth to work at Lifestyle Christianity University (LCU). This move required us to take a pay cut. It was a big move, and after much prayer and many conversations, we decided that we were going to follow the Lord to Texas. I flew in a few months before the move to look for apartments and houses to rent.

I quickly realized that I could not afford to buy or rent a house with my new salary, so I began to look for apartments and settled on one that was one mile from the training center. As I was driving away from the apartment complex the day that I chose the apartment and started filling out the rental application, I said out loud, "Lord, if you can give me a house for my family, that would be amazing." It's like it jumped out of my spirit, as if the Spirit of God spoke through me.

I left the apartment and drove to my first staff meeting at LCU. I was excited to be there and excitedly told the team that I had found a place to rent for my family. I didn't say that I settled on a place to live or that I was looking for something better. I was sitting next to a woman in the meeting. I won't share her name because she would not want anybody to know what she and her husband did for our family. She looked at me. "I think that I have a house for you." My jaw dropped, and she said that she would talk to me about it after the meeting. Since this moment, she and her husband have become our Texas parents.

When the meeting was over, she again looked at me. "Do you want to go see it?" We left and drove to the house, a nice two-story on a cul-de-sac. She walked me through the house. "Do you like it?"

I answered, "Yes, but there is no way that I can afford to live here."

She said, "We can talk about that tonight." Later that night, I met her and her husband for dinner, and they told me that they believed the house was for Chelsea and me. They eventually wanted to sell it to us, but they would start by renting it to us for the same price as the apartment that I was going to rent. And even better, if we had any problem paying the bills, to let them know and they would help us. I was absolutely blown away.

After we had rented the house for about a year, they asked if we were ready to buy it. I didn't think it was possible, but then they said that they were going to gift us a very high amount of equity in the home and that they would pay the down payment for us as well, making it possible for us to buy it. Through them, Jesus made it possible for Chelsea and I to own our first house. To this day, this testimony still shakes me to the core.

Chelsea and I faithfully tithed and gave above that at times. The Lord saw that we were obedient to his Word, so when it was time, he gifted us the perfect house in that season so that we could do the work of ministry that he had for our family in Texas at Lifestyle Christianity. If you are obedient to give, you will experience open rewards.

Prayer

In Matthew 6:6, Jesus says, "But you, when you pray, go into your room, and when you have shut your door, pray to your Father who is in the secret place; and your Father, who sees in secret, will reward you openly" (NKJV). Again he says, "*when* you pray" not *if* you pray. If you don't pray, you will not be rewarded openly. He is an example of an open reward when it comes to prayer.

Every time before we go out on outreach, we pray. We say that prayer is not something that we do before we do something important; prayer is as important as anything else that we are about to do. We also say that we pray to go from our strength into God's strength. So one Wednesday, before outreach, as usual, we prayed our five specific prayers: let us be Spirit-led, atmosphere shifting, and chain breaking, and fill the nets and send the laborers.

After we prayed, we went out in faith to find God's lost kids. We were headed to a certain street in Fort Worth. I took a wrong turn, or so we thought. We have found is that after we pray "Lord, lead us by your Spirit," we often turn right where the Holy Spirit wants us to go, even if we had not planned it. So we ended up on a street and decided to start there.

We started going door to door, and the first house that I walked up to was Samuel's house. When we knocked on the door, he answered, and after we talked for a few minutes about what it means to be born again, he made the decision that day to pray to do so. He went and got his mother to come to the door as well so that she could be there when he prayed. It also happened to be his birthday. How amazing that the Holy Spirit would lead us to his house on his birthday to pray with him to start a relationship with God. His mother told me that he was the oldest of five brothers and that he had always wanted an older brother. Since that day, I have done my best to be that for Samuel. We have gone to a college football bowl game at AT&T Stadium, watched a Texas Rangers major league baseball game, and even taken a trip to Washington state together where I got to see Samuel fly on his first airplane. At the time of writing this book, Samuel just celebrated his one-year spiritual birthday.

You see, if we pray, we will have open rewards from the father. That open reward looks like God adding a spiritual brother to your life named Samuel. I can't imagine my life without Samuel in it. He is truly an open reward to a life of prayer. We must understand that if I never prayed, then this would have never happened. We have to make sure that we are actually doing what Jesus has called us to do. If all I did was read a book on prayer and left it at that, I would have never met Samuel and had the opportunity to lead him to the Lord.

Fasting

Matthew 6:16–18 says, "But you, when you fast, anoint your head and wash your face, so that you do not appear to men to be fasting, but to your Father who is in the secret place; and your Father who sees in secret will reward you openly" (NKJV). Here again, it doesn't say "*if* you fast" but "*when* you fast." We can't have a mentality that thinks we get a reward without doing anything. That's not how it works. If we are going to receive the reward of fasting, then at some point, we will need to say no to food.

I have had many different seasons of fasting, and many more are in front of me. A few years ago, as we were starting the ministry of 33rd Company, we were in a season of fasting as we wanted to hear clearly what the Lord was saying about what he wanted us to build. Around this time, I took a trip to Mississippi to pick up a van from my friend Andrew Barr. He is a crop farmer who has a big heart to see our cities reached for Jesus. He gifted our new ministry a fifteen-passenger Ford Transit van that we are still using to this day to reach the lost.

While in Mississippi with Andrew, we drove by a house with a family out front on the porch. I felt that the Holy Spirit wanted us to stop and talk to them for a moment. So they pulled the van over, and I walked up to the house and began to talk to the family. I asked if any of them needed prayer, and they all pointed to a sixteen-year-old girl sitting on the other side of the porch with her head down. I walked toward her and asked if I could pray for her, but she did not respond. So I asked again, and again, she said nothing. I prayed under my breath, hoping for a shift, and the third time she replied that I could pray for her. I took her hand to pray, and she seemed to encounter the Lord. I then shared the simple gospel with her, and she said, "Yes, I want to be born again." As I took her hand to pray for her to be born again, she began to manifest a demonic spirit. I took authority over it in Jesus's name and told it to leave. It left. She then prayed to be born again.

Matthew 17:21 says, "However, this kind does not go out except by prayer and fasting" (NKJV). Because I was in a season of fasting, my open reward was seeing this girl delivered from demons. I don't want to get into the theology of casting out demons in this book, but if we fast, we have authority to cast out demons. The next day, that girl and her mother joined us for church, and she looked like a completely different person. Jesus is the only one that can save and deliver. If you fast, you will have an open reward, but if you don't fast, then all you have is a theory.

Going, Growing, and Truly Knowing

If we never do his will and go for it, then we will never grow in the things of God. And if we never grow in the things of God, then we will never truly know God as much as he wants us to know him. I'm not saying that we need to grow only in our intellectual understanding of God but in our obedience to God. Many professors and theologians know way more about the Bible than I do, and I respect that they have studied and grown in understanding the Scriptures, but if all that we do is study and never apply what we learn, then we really are not walking in all that God wants us to walk in. Everything in the Christian walk gets to be walked out in our daily lives. That should be exciting. We get to live out what the Word of God calls us to, not just talk about and study it. I study often, but I always try my best to make sure that I daily practice what I'm studying. I want my study to lead to transformation, not information stored in my head. Honestly, we have a lot of studying and not a lot of action in the body of Christ, and we must now begin to go so that we will grow so that we will truly know God.

Just this morning, as I was writing this book in a cabin in Fredericksburg, Texas, with Chelsea, I led the lady who cleans the cabins to the Lord. She was powerfully born again, and felt the Holy Spirit come into her heart when she prayed to be born again. I had gone for a three-mile run, and when I got back to our cabin, she was walking right past my door. Talk about perfect timing. You can't make this stuff up. We are in the middle of nowhere in Texas, and nobody else is out here but us because it's the middle of the week. Alma was in the perfect place for me to share with her what it means to be born again. You see, I can have a theology that Jesus saves and that we are called to be witnesses but never share with a single person. I had to take action and actually go for it and share the gospel with her. The result was that she was born again and given eternal life.

Go So You Will Grow

So many Christians are waiting to be ready and fully equipped before they do anything for the Lord. I'm all about being equipped and trained. That is why we have the fivefold ministry to equip the saints to do the work of ministry, and that is the purpose of this book. But we grow the best when we are actively doing the will of the Father. As a pastor for a few years now, I have talked to many newly married couples who want to have children. They say all the time that they don't think they are ready or prepared to have children and give a long list of what needs to happen before they do so that they are prepared. Now some of the points on their lists are valid, but honestly, most of the points really won't be a make it or break it for having a child. I often tell those that ask me for my advice on timing about this that they will probably never feel fully equipped or prepared to bring that brand-new baby home.

My stomach was twisted in knots the day we drove Ellie home from the hospital. We walked out of the hospital and put that precious gift in the car for the first time. Driving home seemed to take forever and potholes in the road somehow felt like a massive earthquake every time we hit one. *They are letting us take this baby home? I don't know what I'm doing.* Chelsea and I were not professional parents, but we both loved the Lord and knew how to pray. And that's what we did. At the writing of this book, that little baby is now a beautiful eleven-year-old girl. She turned out just fine, and we have three other happy and healthy kids as well. It's called learning on the go.

Many Christians probably know more than they actually think that they know. If they began to step out and share with others, they would realize that they are more prepared than they think they are to be a witness. It's not rocket science at all; it's just understanding the simple truths of who Jesus is. If they would begin to step out, they would also understand that the helper and greatest teacher of all time is there with them like my skydiving instructor was on my back.

John 14:26 says, "But the Helper, the Holy Spirit, whom the Father will send in My name, He will teach you all things, and bring to your remembrance all things that I said to you" (NKJV). This amazing truth reminds us that as we go, we have the Holy Spirit there to help and teach us as we are stepping out in faith. He gives us this beautiful promise in Matthew 28:20. "Teaching them to observe all that I have commanded you. And behold, I am with you always, to the end of the age." He promised us that he would be with us as we go. What more do we need than the Holy Spirit with us as we go out to make disciples and be witnesses for Jesus?

You see, the point is that you will never be fully ready because if you could be fully prepared then you could do it in your own strength. What God has called us to is impossible without him. We have to have him in order to pull it off. Second Corinthians 12:9 says, "But he said to me, "My grace is sufficient for you, for my power is made perfect in weakness. Therefore I will boast all the more gladly of my weaknesses, so that the power of Christ may rest upon me." If you can do it in your strength, then you could also fall into the temptation of taking the glory for what happens. But when you are weak and don't feel totally confident in what the Lord has called you to do, then when he does it through you by his grace, you give him the glory because he was the one that did all the work.

Let's be as equipped as we can be, but let's also understand that at a certain point, we just need to step out in faith and go for it. God is with us and has our backs. The Holy Spirit is looking for people willing to take steps of faith into the unknown and believe that he is there with them. Will you step out and believe God for great demonstrations, or will you just be satisfied with intellectual knowledge? I want to encourage you to step out and believe God for great exploits because the reward of seeing God move through and around you is way more rewarding than sitting on the sidelines (Daniel 11:32).

Let's take a look at Acts 3 and 4 where we see this pattern: going in faith, leading to growing in faith, which then leads to the church truly knowing the faith.

Going

Acts 3 starts with Peter and John walking to the temple to pray. They came across a man who was lame from birth. He was laid daily at the gate called Beautiful. I want to point out the obvious, but they were on their way to the temple to pray. These words of Jesus were on their minds and hearts.

And he said to them, "Go into all the world and proclaim the gospel to the whole creation. Whoever believes and is baptized will be saved, but whoever does not believe will be condemned. And these signs will accompany those who believe: in my name they will cast out demons; they will speak in new tongues; they will pick up serpents with their hands; and if they drink any deadly poison, it will not hurt them; they will lay their hands on the sick, and they will recover. (Mark 16:15–18)

Jesus's words here were not just good theology that they discussed that weekend at Sunday school. They actually walked this out in their daily lives. So when they saw the man lying there, they knew that they could help him because Jesus said that they could.

So in Acts 3:6–7, we find this powerful account. "But Peter said, I have no silver and gold, but what I do have I give to you. In the name of Jesus Christ of Nazareth, rise up and walk! And he took him by the right hand and raised him up, and immediately his feet and ankles were made strong." Peter and John acted on what they had been given, and the result was that the man who was lame was healed and stood up. This is amazing, and this same thing can happen today if we are willing to step out in faith and believe God to move. We can see people healed, saved, and delivered if we simply obey God at his Word and get going.

Growing

Peter and John had this amazing victory that had come through their obedience to Jesus. This miracle caused a lot of attention. The religious leaders were not very happy about it and did not want the disciples teaching in the name of Jesus. In the beginning of Acts 4, those leaders arrested them and put them in jail overnight. When they came back the next day, they warned them to not teach or share about Jesus anymore. They were trying hard to intimidate them and get them to be quiet, but their threats did not work. Peter and John replied in Acts 4:19–21, "But Peter and John answered them, 'Whether it is right in the sight of God to listen to you rather than to God, you must judge, for we cannot but speak of what we have seen and heard.' And when they had further threatened them, they let them go, finding no way to punish them, because of the people, for all were praising God for what had happened."

I love this testimony because Peter and John grew in God through their obedience. They acted because "of what we have seen and heard." When they stepped out in faith, they saw a miracle of God happen in front of their eyes and thus grew in confidence and boldness. If you see a man get up and walk who has been lame for years, that will affect your faith. You see, many Christians don't step out in faith, so they don't grow in God.

Let's go there for a minute. In 2020, when the US government said the churches had to social distance, not meet for worship, and wear masks, many shrank back and did what they were told. Why? Because they had not seen the sick healed, the lost saved, and the blind receive their sight. The kingdom of God is meant to be seen and heard, not talked about and discussed. All many had was a theory and not a kingdom reality. The moment the threat came, they backed into the corner and said yes to whatever the government demanded. Because Peter and John stepped out, they personally grew in the things of God. But not only did they grow in their faith but their act of faith and demonstration of the miraculous power of God caused other believers to grow as well.

> When they were released, they went to their friends and reported what the chief priests and the elders had said to them. And when they heard it, they lifted their voices together to God and said, "Sovereign Lord, who made the heaven and the earth and the sea and everything in them, who through the mouth of our father David, your servant, said by the Holy Spirit, "'Why did the Gentiles rage, and the peoples plot in vain? The kings of the earth set themselves, and the rulers were gathered together, against the Lord and against his Anointed'—for truly in this city there were gathered together against your holy servant Jesus, whom you anointed, both Herod and Pontius Pilate, along with the Gentiles and the peoples of Israel, to do whatever your hand and your plan had predestined to take place. And now, Lord, look upon their threats and grant to your servants to continue to speak your word with all boldness, while you stretch out

your hand to heal, and signs and wonders are performed through the name of your holy servant Jesus." And when they had prayed, the place in which they were gathered together was shaken, and they were all filled with the Holy Spirit and continued to speak the word of God with boldness. (Acts 4:23–31)

When the others heard about their boldness, obedience, and the miracle, boldness rose within them. Our obedience and yes to God inspires others to give their yes to God. I want to live a life that motivates others to pray for boldness so that they go out and speak the word of God fearlessly. I pray that you are convicted of the same thing. Take what the Lord has given you and the understanding that he is with you and step out because your friends and family are going to grow as you go. Your victories become their victories.

Truly Know

When we as the church begin to live this way, we will begin to focus on what really matters and will quit dividing over issues that don't matter at all. When we daily begin to see and hear the kingdom of God all around us, we will begin to truly know what matters most to Jesus and have true unity in the body of Christ. People are splitting hairs on the second coming of Christ, and I'm over here trying to break chains so that he will return. Because we know one thing for a fact: He will come when the gospel of the kingdom is preached to all people and nations.(Matthew 24:14). You see, if all we have is theory and intellectual arguments, the church will remain divided. But if we have a kingdom reality, and are seeing people saved, healed, and delivered weekly, we are going to be less likely to split over the color of the chairs in our new church building.

If we begin to truly know the power of God in our daily lives, then we will see unity in the church like never before. Acts 4:32 says, "Now the full number of those who *believed were of one heart and soul*, and no one said that any of the things that belonged to him was his own, but they had everything in common" (emphasis added). They were of one heart and soul; they were in it together because they were under the lordship of Jesus and were experiencing the kingdom of God expanding in front of their eyes. If we as individuals begin to start going with our faith, then we will begin to grow personally, and our growth will cause those around us to grow. When we all are growing and experiencing the kingdom and not arguing over theories and doctrines, we will then begin to truly know the Lord and have real unity.

One last practical point to understand about this concept is that as you go in the little areas, you will grow into bigger areas. Many people don't ever step out because they are so overwhelmed with the thought and task at hand that they don't ever get started. Don't be overwhelmed. You don't have to start at the gate called Beautiful and try to see a lame man walk. You can start by simply smiling at the person next to you and saying "Jesus loves you." When I'm about to send people on outreach, I often say, "If all you do on this outreach is think about sharing your faith with somebody, we will celebrate that you thought about it because many believers don't even think about it, let alone show up to an outreach." We will celebrate the fact that you simply showed up. Step two is to walk up to somebody and hand them a church card and run away. We will celebrate that as well. I'm joking, but I'm trying to make a point. You have to start somewhere, so just start, and as you start, you will begin to grow. I promise you.

I did not start sharing my faith in Japan, Iraq, Pakistan, and Israel but in Walmart, Target, and Costco. Just simply give God your yes and watch how much you quickly grow. Maturity in the kingdom of God has little to do with your age and a lot to do with your obedience. You could be seventy-five years old, not step out in obedience, and be immature in sharing your faith. You could be twenty years old and step out every time the Holy Spirit speaks. You are more mature and growing at a much faster rate.

So as Christians, we want to be growing daily. That means that we need to be living in constant obedience to the Holy Spirit. Not enough church outreaches happen weekly that we can join to grow like we need to be growing. The good news is that we don't need to be on an outreach to share our faith. We can share our faith as we go.

In the next chapter, I will talk about how our mission is wherever our feet are. This next chapter will change your life if you read it and decide to turn your whole life into a mission trip. I would encourage you to do that because there is no better way to live. You can get activated through outreaches so that you become a full-time Christian everywhere you go.

9

YOUR MISSION IS WHERE YOUR FEET ARE

We, as believers, need to live in the present with God. That's all that we have. The past and future are important, but we can't live there. We should remember the past and learn from all that we have gone through: the good, the bad and the in-between. We should be excited about the future and all that it holds and believe in God for great things. But we need to truly live in the here and now.

The Past

Many people are stuck in the past. Maybe it's what others have done to them, or maybe it's what they did to others that they can't seem to get past. They end up living in a place of guilt, shame, and condemnation that causes them to be stuck and to think that they are unqualified to be used by God. This is such an absolute lie from the pit of hell to sideline people. Philippians 3:13–14 says, "No, dear brothers and sisters, I have not achieved it, but I focus on this one thing: Forgetting the past and looking forward to what lies ahead, I press on to reach the end of the race and receive the heavenly prize for which God, through Christ Jesus, is calling us" (NLT).

We need to forget the past and look forward to what is ahead. What does God have for you today? How does God want to use you today? What does the Lord have for you to do today? If we are stuck in the past, then we will never step into what God has for us today. Another Scripture that is so important to remember and keep before us is "So now there is no condemnation for those who belong to Christ Jesus. And because you belong to him, the power of the life-giving Spirit has freed you from the power of sin that leads to death" (Romans 8:1–2 NLT).

This Scripture is so powerful. If you belong to Christ, then you are free because his life-giving Spirit has freed you from the power of sin. If you are reading this book and believe that Jesus is Lord and confess that with your life, then you are counted as one that belongs to him. And if you belong to him, then you are free in him. Second Corinthians 3:17 says, "Now the Lord is the Spirit, and where the Spirit of the Lord is, there is freedom." This means that you are not bound by your past mistakes or sins, but you can be free in Christ if you give your life to him and completely surrender yourself to his lordship. We can't come to him halfway and expect to be free; we have to completely come into the light so that we can fully know him and be known.

This process of navigating our past can take time, which I understand. God is patient and kind with us on our journey to freedom in Christ. I just want to make sure that you are not stuck, thinking that you will never truly be free, because that lie needs to be broken. You can be free and will be free if you seek first the kingdom of God and don't ever look back. There are many great books on freedom and deliverance, and you should read them on your journey to freedom in Christ, but don't allow those books and YouTube channels to take the place of Jesus and his presence. Daily encounters with Jesus and the presence of God will set you free. There is no ten-step plan; it's one step: Jesus. Jesus is salvation, Jesus is deliverance, Jesus is healing, Jesus is peace, and Jesus is hope. If we have Jesus and his presence, then we have all that we need. Make sure that you take time to be in his presence daily. That is the only way to get free and stay free.

People also get stuck in the past in the good old glory days. Many of us know a person like that who always brings up what the Lord did twenty or thirty years ago. Those stories are great the first few times that you hear them, and we want to honor what the Lord has done in the past. Yes, I am standing on the shoulders of those that went before me, but at the same time, I want God to move today. I want a testimony of what God did through me today by his grace and power. We need to remember all that God has done in the past but live in the present moment with God. If God did it back then, then he is more than able to do it again today.

It's not out with the old and in with the new. So many young leaders have made this mistake and pushed the old traditions and ways out for so-called new ways. Really, there is only one way, and his name is Jesus. We must understand that God has been restoring the church back to her full glory. In the 1500s, Martin Luther restored Jesus and grace back to the church. In the early 1900s, the Welsh and Azusa Street revivals restored the Holy Spirit back to the church. In the 1990s, the Toronto outpouring restored the Father's love back to the church. Many refer to this outpouring as "The Father's blessing." During many other moves of God throughout history, the Lord has revealed truths to the church that are very common to us today. In the 1960s, Lonnie Frisbee was used powerfully in the Jesus People movement to awaken the church to power evangelism in the streets.

I want to be a Christian that knows and honors the past but is not missing out on what the Lord is doing today. God is moving today and is looking to use people that are open and available. In this season, God is doing many things in the church, including awakening the church to what it looks like to live on mission everywhere you go. In times past, the focus was on the man or woman of God moving in the power of God in a church setting. But a shift is coming, a shift where God is using every person in the body of Christ to minister everywhere they go. Can you imagine every Christian always living on mission? Every Christian would have the compassion of Jesus in their hearts, the power of God in their hands, and the gospel ready to be preached in their mouths. How amazing! We are moving away from superstar

Christianity to full-body ministry. We are all called to walk this out and live a life that is always on mission.

If you're reading this and you are stuck in the good old days, I want to encourage you to grow in this season. People's lives depend upon it. I was visiting one of our internship locations, spending time with a group of interns talking about evangelism and discipleship. A man and his wife were there; she was doing the internship. He was a good sport about her doing the internship, but he wanted nothing to do with what I was saying. You could tell by his body language. At the end of the time together, he said to the whole group, "There is no way that I will ever do what you are talking about."

You could have heard a pin drop. The whole group waited for my response. I thought for a moment and decided that a bold comment like that deserved an equally bold comment back. "So you want to live in disobedience to God and his Word?" There was an awkward silence. We were in a standoff. By the end of the night, we were sitting together at dinner and had a wonderful time together. I share this story to give you an example of how many think. Even some reading this book probably may have thought this way in the past or still do today. But it's time to shake off the old ways that are holding you back and step into the new. The Lord has new wine for you, and the truth is that the new wine he has for you is amazing.

"And it shall come to pass afterward that I will pour out My Spirit on all flesh; Your sons and your daughters shall prophesy, your old men shall dream dreams, your young men shall see visions. Also, on my menservants and on my maidservants I will pour out my Spirit in those days" (Joel 2:28–29 NKJV).

God has poured out his Spirit on all Christians. The passage says all flesh; that means all flesh. God didn't just pour out his Spirit on some well-known ministers who are super gifted and have a large social media following. I can't say this loudly enough: *all flesh*! Please don't buy the lie from the enemy that your past disqualifies you, and please don't get stuck in the way it was. Ask God for the new wine and watch what he begins to do through you. When you begin to live every day on mission with Jesus, you won't live in the past. You will be too busy with what he wants to do through you today.

The Future

Okay, we talked about getting over the hurdles of the past. Now, let's talk about the hurdles of the future. The future can be just as much of a problem for people as the past can.

Some people live in constant fear and anxiety of the future and what it holds. They get wound up so tightly that they can't just live in the moment with God and enjoy the ride. Tragically, when people are in this place of fear, it paralyzes them and keeps them from living their life to the fullest today. So much is unknown, and that's okay, because we have a God who promises to take care of us day by day and moment by moment. Jesus knew that we humans would struggle with this, so he talked about it. It is recorded in Matthew 6. Read the full passage below slowly and ask the Lord to deliver you of any fear about the future.

"That is why I tell you not to worry about everyday life— whether you have enough food and drink, or enough clothes to wear. Isn't life more than food, and your body more than clothing? Look at the birds. They don't plant or harvest or store food in barns, for your heavenly Father feeds them. And aren't you far more valuable to him than they are? Can all your worries add a single moment to your life? And why worry about your clothing? Look at the lilies of the field and how they grow. They don't work or make their clothing, yet Solomon in all his glory, was not dressed as beautifully as they are. And if God cares so wonderfully for wildflowers that are here today and thrown into the fire tomorrow, he will certainly care for you. Why do you have so little faith? So don't worry about these things, saying, 'What will we eat? What will we drink? What will we wear?' These things dominate the thoughts of unbelievers, but your heavenly Father already knows all your needs. Seek the kingdom of God above all else, and live righteously, and he will give you everything you need. So don't worry about tomorrow, for tomorrow will bring its own worries. Today's trouble is enough for today." (Matthew 6:25–34 NLT)

He promises that he will give us everything that we need. What an amazing promise from the Lord. I have memorized Matthew 6:33 and repeat it daily to myself as I go about my day. His promises are true to us and we have nothing to fear if we are seeking first his kingdom. Jesus says that these fears dominate the lives of unbelievers. If you are born again, you are a believer. But I fear that many have fallen into the trap of what I call the unbelieving believer. This person says Jesus is Lord, but their life is not dominated by his promises but by the thoughts and fears of this world. I want to call you higher because if we are going to live every day on mission, then we are going to need to trust God with our lives.

I have also seen people get so worried about what their next season in life will be. Where should they move? What should they do? What church should they attend? Who should they marry? Should they go to college? Should they pursue full-time ministry or a different career? And the questions go on and on. These are all great questions and important. Pray and fast to get the answers from God, but please don't live so much in the future and be so consumed by what will come that you miss out on the moment today. I pray about my future and make plans according to what I hear the Lord say, but I don't allow the future to move me from living on mission with Jesus today.

At the beginning of 2023, the Lord spoke to Chelsea and I about 2024, and we have shifted our schedule and life to accommodate what the Lord said to do. He said, "Don't travel for a year, slow down, and reach as many people as you can in Fort Worth, Waco, and Dallas," so that is what I'm going to do. I'm all about hearing from the Lord and obeying, and trust me, the Lord will speak to you about your future. It will be amazing when he does, but please don't focus so much on it that you miss out on today.

When I take Chelsea to lunch, we will minister to our server, like we always do, because we live on mission, not in the future. We will talk about the future today and be excited about what is to come, but we understand this Scripture well.

"We can make our plans, but the Lord determines our steps" (Proverbs 16:9 NLT). The Lord ultimately determines our steps. This brings me so much peace, knowing that if I fear the Lord and seek to please God, he will ultimately cause me to end up where I need to be. I don't have time to share with you all the times that I thought that I confidently had the next steps figured out but realized that the step that I thought was certain was actually just a step to get me to where God ultimately wanted me to be. He has a way of getting us where he needs us when he needs us there, and I rest in that truth. Plan for the future, but hold on to those plans lightly because he has way bigger and better plans than anything that you can dream up on your own.

I want to talk to the young and adventurous eighteen-to-thirty-year-olds for a moment. You are going to change the world, and it's going to be amazing. But we change the world by changing the world around us today. I have talked to many of you on my global travels, and I love your fire and passion for Jesus. Just please make sure that you are living out your faith today and not waiting for your big ministry moment or missionary call to the nations.

Listen, I say this all the time. It's not going to be glamorous, but it will be glorious. Don't be fooled thinking that once you get to the mission field or paid on the church staff that you will start your ministry. That is not one bit true. Your ministry starts today. What are you doing with what God has given you today? You won't preach the gospel in Pakistan when you get there if you won't share the gospel at Walmart when you get there today. You see, young people, this is the problem with the American church today. We have too many professional pulpit preachers and social media influencers that are scared to share their faith at Walmart because they really aren't ministers of the gospel. They are just church entertainers at best. I don't want you to be a church entertainer. I want you to be a full-time, sold-out witness for the Lord who changes the world everywhere you go. That only takes place if the Lord develops you in the secret place and the workplace before he releases you into public ministry. So please embrace the process that God has you in today as you go from place to place. He can then send you to the nations and into full-time ministry so that when you get there, you will actually be effective for his kingdom. Don't get ahead of yourself. Kill some lions and bears first before you go after a Goliath.

"Don't worry about this Philistine," David told Saul. "I'll go fight him!" "Don't be ridiculous!" Saul replied. "There's no way you can fight this Philistine and possibly win! You're only a boy, and he's been a man of war since his youth." But David persisted. "I have been taking care of my father's sheep and goats," he said. "When a lion or a bear comes to steal a lamb from the flock, I go after it with a club and rescue the lamb from its mouth. If the animal turns on me, I catch it by the jaw and club it to death. I have done this to both lions and bears, and I'll do it to this pagan Philistine, too, for he has defied the armies of the living God! The Lord who rescued me from the claws of the lion and the bear will rescue me from this Philistine!" Saul finally consented. "All right, go ahead," he said. "And may the Lord be with you!" (1 Samuel 17:32–37 NLT)

David had history with God. The God who delivered him from the lion and bear would certainly deliver him from Goliath. We need to build a history with God. One day, I was flying to Israel to minister in Nazareth. and on the plane ride, the Holy Spirit said, "I'm sending you to my hometown because you stewarded your hometown."

What a moment! Because I killed lions and bears in Woodland, the Lord was sending me to Nazareth to confront a giant. What you do today matters, so do something great for God, which will open doors of opportunity for you to do even greater exploits tomorrow.

I was talking to a young lady who had returned to her hometown from YWAM. She was so concerned about her future and the specific ministry that the Lord was calling her to. She was away from all the excitement of YWAM after a few months. She was frustrated and wanted to be powerfully used by God, which was great. She had true passion for Jesus even though she was off in her thinking a bit. As I began to talk to her, I told her that she didn't need to wait for her next mission trip to be used by God. She could turn her hometown into a mission field. This subtle shift in perspective brought such clarity to her. She began to get excited about her home church and hometown. If she stewarded her hometown with great faith and expectation, the nations would open to her. She began to cry and thanked me for sharing that simple truth with her. I want to share this same truth with you: Slow down and enjoy the ride. The only reason that I'm where I am today is because I stewarded where I was yesterday and the day before that: sharing my faith on the dairy farm, at Rain City pressure washing, at the feed store, at the construction site, and at restaurants, stores and other establishments around the community. This built in me the grit that I need to share the gospel in Iraq, Pakistan, Israel, and the nations.

A team of us were in Pakistan a few years back. We were sitting around a table with the leaders, getting to know them for the first time in person. We now do life and ministry with those same leaders, our Pakistani family. We had been with them for a few days and were talking about that day's ministry plan. As we ended, the conversation took a turn. One of them very politely said to me, "Chris, we want you to know that you are free to do what you want, but we want to ask you to please not share your faith everywhere that you go."

They were talking about at the gas station, restaurant, and while walking from place to place. I have never liked that word *but*, but they were polite in their request. They had a good reason: As my hosts, they wanted to keep me safe and protect me. But I can hear fear when it's talking. We can often hide fear behind what appears to be wisdom. I asked them a question. "If Jesus were here, would you ask him to do the same thing?"

They put their heads down for a moment and looked back up. "No, we would not ask Jesus to do the same thing."

I then said, "Well, Jesus is here in each one of you around this table. I don't think that we should hold him back. Do you?" And they agreed that I was right and that they were just dealing with fear in stepping out themselves. That moment brought such a shift to all those around the table.

Since that day, they love it when we step out, and they step out as well. If I had not been a Christian in the States, living every day on mission with Jesus, I would have listened to them and been quiet. But since I live every day in obedience to God, my breakthrough back home became a breakthrough for Pakistan. You see, every nation has its culture and reasons that hold back

Christians from stepping out, but we should not be moved by the culture of the nation that we find ourselves in. We should be moved by heaven's culture. Again, the lions and bears that I took down in my hometown helped me face a Goliath in Pakistan.

Mission Trip, Faith, and Expectation

Have you ever wondered why God moves so powerfully on church mission trips but not in your home cities? So many times, a team from church will head to another nation, and when they get back home, they are so energized by what God has done. This excitement normally wears off after a few weeks, and life often goes back to the way that it was before: church on Sunday and work Monday through Friday.

It doesn't have to be that way. You can live on mission at home just as much as you do on a mission trip to Japan or China. God moves on mission trips because those that go often have an expectation that God will move through them. What if we lived with that same expectation today at our job or schools? God is the same in Texas as he is in Sweden. People need salvation as much in Washington State as they do in Florida. People need healing in Kentucky as much as they do Kenya. You see, it comes down to whether we are living with faith and expectations that God is going to move today.

On any given Saturday morning when I wake up and Chelsea asks me to run to the store to pick up some waffle mix for the family, all of heaven begins to move and stir. Can you see it? I step out of the house, half asleep with a coffee in my hand, and the angels in heaven begin to talk. "Hey, guys, this was not on his calendar, so we were not prepared, but Chelsea decided to send him to the store to pick up waffle mix. We need to get ready for anything." Why is there movement in heaven? Because when God speaks, I obey.

As I'm driving to the store, the angels are working overtime to set up divine encounters for when I get there. When I park my truck, open the door, and step out of the vehicle, all of hell screams because they know that an obedient son just arrived on the scene. I walk in and go to aisle 10, and as I find the waffle mix, the voice of

God says, "Ask that lady next to you if the name *Vicki* means anything to her."

I ask, and the lady almost falls over because Vicki is her best friend in the hospital fighting for her life. These kinds of stories happen all the time, almost every week. Why? Because I live with faith and expectancy that God wants to work through me. This is normal Christianity. Not clocking in and out and trying to be a good person. We are called to change the world daily by hearing the voice of God and stepping out in obedience.

When you step out the door, is heaven moved to attention, knowing that you are obedient and will say yes to what the Holy Spirit asks you to do? Many of us, like the man that I shared about at the internship gathering, have already told the Lord no. Then we wonder why he doesn't do these same miracles daily through us that he does through others. You may need to take a minute to repent to the Lord and say you're sorry for saying no even before he speaks. Take some time to count the cost, and give Jesus your yes, so when he speaks, you will say yes automatically.

One day, Chelsea and I went to Best Buy in Portland. As we were there shopping, I walked by a man and his wife and got a word of knowledge for her. I turned around and asked her if she was having any difficulty in her shoulder because the Lord seemed to highlight that to me. They were both shocked. She said, "Yes, we just left the doctor's office where they ran tests to figure out what is going on. A mass on my shoulder is causing pain." I asked if I could pray for them, and they agreed. I prayed a very simple prayer and asked the Lord to heal her. We had a bit of small talk after I prayed. She was a Christian and her husband grew up in a home where his father was Muslim and his mother was Catholic. He later became an atheist and did not have faith in anything. I told them my name and what church I went to and then went about my day with Chelsea. I knew that it was a divine encounter but didn't know where it would lead.

A few months later, I received a message through Facebook messenger from this woman's sister. "Is this the Chris Donald that prayed for my sister in Best Buy a few months ago? If it is, I want you to know that after you prayed for her, all the pain left, and the lump went away. She is trying to get ahold of you because her husband is in the hospital on life support. If you can come to the hospital to pray for him, she would really appreciate that."

The next day, I drove to the hospital to pray for him and asked God to do a miracle in his body. As I walked into the waiting room, the entire family was there, and I began to minister to them all as the Spirit led. I got a word of knowledge for one of his brothers and prayed for him, and he was healed and had an encounter with the Lord right there. God was moving, and I could clearly see that the step of obedience in Best Buy was opening up to be much more than I expected. The Muslim father took me back to his son to pray for him to be healed in Jesus's name. I prayed and believed God to raise him up. A day later, he passed away. We don't know where he is today for certain, but his wife believes that the day at Best Buy opened his eyes to see Jesus for who he really is. Regardless, her faith grew, and she come back to Lord and is hopeful that he believed as well since they talked about Jesus multiple times after she was healed. We honestly won't know until the other side.

The family asked if I would do the funeral. I was blown away by this. I had only met them two months ago in Best Buy and visited them at the hospital, but God had his plans and wanted me to do this funeral. The funeral was large with around 350–400 people. I got up and said, "You are probably wondering who I am. My name is Chris, and one day I was in Best Buy and God healed this woman's shoulder." I never would have thought that living on mission at Best Buy would put me in a place to be a witness for Jesus at a funeral full of people, half of them Catholics and half of them Muslims. But God knew. You don't know what the Lord has in store for you today. Simply live on mission and obey the Holy Spirit when he speaks to you.

Often, God wants to speak to us, more than we even want to listen at times. For example, when you listen to an old radio, you must tune into the station you want. God is constantly speaking and wants us to tune in, but we are often not on the same radio channel. We are just trying to get in and out of the store as quickly as possible and don't slow down long enough to listen to what the Holy Spirit is saying. He is speaking if we will listen. I often joke with people. "Please listen more so that he will stop talking to me so much." Don't believe the lie that he is not speaking today. He is, and he is waiting for you to learn his voice so that you can begin to reach out to those around you.

One day that Chelsea and I went to IKEA in Portland. We had to return something before we started shopping, so I went to the return counter. As soon as I walked up to the counter, the Lord spoke to me about the lady's back who was helping me with the return. I was so confident that it was the Lord that I said to the woman, "God spoke to me about your back, and he is healing you right now." I didn't even pray. I just spoke what the Lord said.

She instantly felt the Holy Spirit and started getting hot. She took off her outer coat because she was getting so warm and said that her back felt better. She then began to tell me all the problems that were going wrong in her life and all the areas that she needed freedom in. I ministered to her right there in the IKEA return line.

God is always speaking; the question is, are you listening? We learn to hear the voice of God over time, and many teachings and resources out there will help you grow in this area. But honestly, it's quite easy. The Holy Spirit is the best Teacher and will teach you how to hear the voice of God clearly. John 10:27 says, "My sheep listen to my voice; I know them, and they follow me" (NLT). You can hear his voice and follow him. You just need to slow down and listen and determine in your heart that when he speaks, you will obey.

Will You Be the Answer to Someone's Prayer?

People are praying all over our cities and crying out for God to reveal himself to them. Many Christian mothers and grandmothers are praying that God will reach their prodigal kids, grandchildren, husbands, and loved ones. Many times, I was used to answer someone's prayer. It's so amazing when you realize that God used you to do that. When you begin to understand that prayers go up and God is looking for people to carry them out, it changes the way that you go throughout your day. Your day becomes a mission field for God to encounter people. He will begin to set up encounters for you, often because he knows that you won't miss them.

I first began to understand this concept as I kept sharing with husbands and wives while at the store. Over and over again, the wife was saved and the husband was not and was really not interested in talking about Jesus. This finally clicked. I was at Safeway talking to a couple, and the woman said happily, "I'm a believer," and the husband said, "Not me."

My next statement came right out of my spirit. "Oh, I'm sure that your wife has been praying for you." I kid you not, she took a step behind him, put her hands together in the praying position, and mouthed, "Please tell him."

I said to him, "Well, I'm the answer to your wife's prayer. God sent me because I'm a stubborn dairy farmer who is going to tell you the truth." The man was not open at all, but I'm sure that the seeds of the gospel did something in his heart that day. Every time he tried to move, his wife moved, and we boxed him in so he could not leave. After that encounter, I began to see over and over that I was the answer to somebody's prayer.

Another time, I was flying home from the Philippines. We had an amazing mission trip, but that never ends. We are sharing all the time while traveling through airports. As I was walking to my gate, I looked over at a man waiting for his flight. I stopped to talk to him. He was from China and spoke very good English. He was flying from the Philippines back to China. I asked if he was a believer in Jesus, and he said no. Then the Spirit led me to ask if his wife was a believer, and he said yes. I knew at that moment that she had been praying for him. I said to him, "She has been praying for you to have faith in Jesus, hasn't she?" He nodded. I shared with him that I was the answer to her prayer. He sat up and was very engaged in the conversation. After sharing the gospel with him, he chose to be born again and put his faith in Jesus. He boarded the plane back to his wife, a saved man.

Again, why did this happen? Because I was living on mission and God sent me to be the answer to his wife's prayers.

I will end this chapter with one more story that so powerfully shows you that prayers go up and that God is looking for believers like you and me to carry out these prayer requests. On Thursday afternoon, our team gathered to pray before we went to the city to find the one that God was going to lead us to. I prayed, "God, lead me to the one that is ready to encounter you and be born again." We then took off on outreach. We decided to head to North East Mall because my friend David owed me a hat. He had bet me that the Eagles were going to beat the Chiefs in the Super Bowl. The Chiefs won, so I thought, *Let's go on outreach and get a new hat at the same time.*

We went to Lids, and they were closed for some reason, so we decided to walk to the food court and get some food before we tried the hat store again. We only had a short time until we had to head back to the church for Belong. As I was walking toward the Chick-fil-A at the food court, I stopped at a table that Kaden was sitting at with his brother. I simply asked them if I could share the gospel with them. Kaden said yes, so I sat down and shared John 3:1–6 and then explained to them what it meant to be born again. Kaden said yes to Jesus that day and prayed right there to be born again and start a relationship with Jesus. I got his information and said that I would call him after I got back from a trip to Brazil. I was leaving the next day to go to Brazil for a City Quake.

The next day Kaden wrote me and asked if he could come over and get a Bible and some discipleship materials. He knew that I was leaving that day but really wanted to come and get the Bible. When he arrived, he told me that Monday he kneeled for the first time in a long time and prayed. "God, many people ask you for a sign. I'm not asking for a sign. I'm asking that you send me a person." Three days later, God sent me as the answer to that prayer, and Kaden is now a part of my family. He is saved, filled with the Holy Spirit, and actively sharing his faith with others because I was living on mission at the mall and was looking to be an answer to a prayer that somebody prayed that day.

Will you choose to live on a mission? Will you choose to tune into the voice of God? Will you live with faith and expectation that God wants to move through you today? Will you give God your yes? People's lives depend upon it. This can begin to feel heavy, which is why we'll talk about how evangelism is easy in the presence of God in the next chapter. Living this kind of life cannot be done in your own strength and gifting but can only happen if you are living daily in the presence of God.

10

EVANGELISM IS EASY

I have had the honor of taking a lot of people out on their first outreach as I travel the country and different nations. I almost always hear the same thing after we talk to the first few people. They say something like, "This is way easier than I thought it would be." It's true, evangelism is easy in the presence of God. People are very intimidated by the thought of talking to somebody about Jesus whether a family member, coworker, or stranger at the store. But when you know that the Holy Spirit is with you, then what seems difficult becomes easy with him.

Matthew 28:20 says it so clearly. "Teaching them to observe all that I have commanded you. And behold, *I am with you always, to the end of the age*" (emphasis added). What more do we need than the Holy Spirit with us? God told us to go and be witnesses and make disciples of all nations, which is a big task, but he promised us that he would be with us as we do it. Another Scripture that helps drive this home is Luke 24:49.

Jesus said that he was sending the promise of the Father and that promise was to clothe us with the power of the Holy Spirit. You have the Holy Spirit in you for you and on you for others. The Holy Spirit is in you and on you to be a witness to those around you. That means that sharing your faith is only hard when you are doing it in your own strength and intellect. I want to invite you into being a witness for Jesus in his strength and not your own. It's simple. You just have to trust, step out in faith, and go for it. Many are thinking there has to be more to it, but I'm here to tell you there isn't. Just trust God, step out, and see what happens. Remember, you won't grow unless you go.

I was in Billings this past year and was paired up to go on outreach with Angie, age seventy-eight. She had wanted to share her faith for years but never did because she was intimidated by the thought of stepping out and talking to people. She told me in the car on the way that she was so excited that she finally was going out. She was from the Lutheran church in town, and somebody invited her to the event, so she was not even from the church that was hosting me.

We decided to get pizza at Your Pie and shared with a few different people on our way into the restaurant. She just lit up when I began to share. We asked the young man that brought the pizza to our table if we could pray for him, and he said yes and excitedly sat down. He was trying to get closer to God and said he really needed the encouragement and prayer. He was so moved that he teared up as we prayed. When he walked away, Angie looked at me. "This is so easy!"

We then went to Barnes & Noble to look at some books and continue to do outreach. Right before we left, Angie walked over to a young man. He was with another woman on the outreach with us, and she started the conversation with the young man. In just one short outreach, Angie was activated and ready to begin to share her faith on a daily basis. Why? Because she grew in understanding that the Holy Spirit is with us and that he makes evangelism easy.

While I was in Florida building a new believers group for a local church, we spent a day equipping the church staff to go out and share their faith. The worship leader and production lead went with me that day. We had a wonderful time going out and sharing with people. That day, the staff saw eight people born again in ninety minutes of outreach. I had equipped the team with the gospel guide tool, a simple way to start a gospel conversation.

A few months later, early one morning, the worship leader was flying back home from another state. He was really tired and didn't really want to talk to the Uber driver. But the moment he put his guitar in the car, sat down, and shut the door, the driver said, "You play music? I do too" and picked up his drum sticks to show that he was a drummer. Then the driver asked, "Do you have any music that you can show me?"

The worship leader said, "Yeah, check out this song on Spotify." It was a worship song, and the driver turned it on and began to tell him that he was a Muslim. As the song began to play, the presence of God filled the car, and the driver began to cry. The worship leader thought, *Oh no, I need to share the gospel with this guy, but I don't know how.*

He then remembered that I had trained him a few months prior with the gospel guide. He went to my website and pulled it up. The driver couldn't see that he was looking it up, so he thought, *I will just read the card to him.* As he read the card, the guy was ready to be saved. He asked if he would like to be born again, and the driver said yes.

As they pulled up to the airport, he prayed with the driver to be born again and began to disciple him right there by telling him that he would need to share with his family that he made a decision to follow Jesus. The driver agreed and said that he would. This story is another perfect example of evangelism being easy when the presence of God is there.

The Lord of the Harvest

Jesus is the Lord of the harvest. When we understand this, it really removes the pressure off us and allows us to simply trust in God. Here are four very important truths to remember when it comes to evangelism and discipleship.

The Lord Draws Them

John 6:44 says, "For no one can come to me unless the Father, who sent me, draws them to me, and at the last day I will raise them up" (NLT). This truth is so wonderful when you realize that you are looking for people who are ready and have been responding to his call. He is calling all people to himself, but some are responding more than others, and we are out looking for those who are ready to take the next step into a relationship with Jesus.

"The Lord is not slow to fulfill his promise as some count slowness, but is patient toward you, not wishing that any should perish, but that all should reach repentance" (2 Peter 3:9).

This Scripture reveals that God is calling all people to repentance and relationship with him. As people that are out looking to be used by God daily, we just need to be sensitive to know what stage each person is at. When we understand that it's not our responsibility to save anybody but the Lord's, then we can take a deep breath and relax, knowing that he is the Lord of the Harvest.

I was in downtown Fort Worth one day, sharing my faith, and a man walked by named Griffin. He said to me that he had been thinking a lot about God lately and that he was thankful that I was there. We had a great conversation, and I could tell that the Lord had been drawing Griffin and that he had been responding. I shared John 3 with him, and right there in front of the convention center downtown we prayed together so that he could start a relationship with God. To this day, we still keep in touch. He has since moved but is still growing in his relationship with God. This is an example of meeting a person that the Holy Spirit had been drawing to himself.

We Plant and Water

"I *planted*, Apollos *watered*, but God gave the growth" (1 Corinthians 3:6, emphasis added).

One of our jobs as Christians is to plant seeds and water the seeds that others have planted into the hearts of people. Planting and watering seeds can look like many different things: praying for somebody, doing an act of kindness or generosity, being kind and full of the fruit of the Holy Spirit, or inviting someone to church. All of these and many more are examples of how we as Christians should be planting and watering seeds of the gospel in people's hearts. Every encounter is an opportunity to plant and water; that is why it's so important that we are patient and kind with all people that we work with and interact with. When you go out to lunch on Sunday after church, make sure you are nice to your server and ask if you can pray for them because many Christians before you have planted seeds, and we need to make sure to keep planting and watering. We also want to make sure that we are not a bad example of what a Christian is, so please be on your best behavior because you are representing Christians everywhere. We don't have the best reputation already, so please help us change that.

Chelsea and I were at Target coming through the self-checkout line, and the lady that was there to assist that line came up to Chelsea. "I just had to come over here and tell you that you are just the nicest and sweetest family that comes through this Target. Every time I see you, it just makes my day."

Chelsea responded, "Let me tell you why. It's because of Jesus." This is a perfect example of planting and watering seeds. Every time Chelsea went to Target, she was planting seeds into this woman's heart without even trying. She was just kind and full of the fruit of the Holy Spirit. When the woman came and talked to her about what she had witnessed by being around Chelsea and the family, Chelsea then watered that seed by saying "It's Jesus," with a smile on her face.

We are called to plant and water seeds in people's lives. And we must remember that we are doing this in every conversation and interaction with the people that we are around. Be a Christian that plants and waters often.

We Reap

"I sent you to *reap* that for which you did not labor. Others have labored, and you have entered into their labor." (John 4:38, emphasis added).

The church really needs to grow in this area. We need to become Christians who don't just plant and water but who want to reap the harvest that is ready today. People in your cities today are ready to start a relationship with Jesus. All that we need to do is be there to ask them if they are ready and then lead them through the simple steps to start that relationship and be willing to disciple them after they are born again.

I regularly equip at our church's Leadership School on Wednesdays before we go out on outreach. I start the school year talking about our need to be reaping evangelists and then equip the class with a few very simple Scriptures and questions that they can ask people to see if they are ready. I want the students to not only look to plant and water but also to reap.

One Wednesday, after we got back from an outreach, I was in my car on a phone call. An SLS student came up to my car. I rolled down the window, and she excitedly said, "Six people were born again today on outreach. I had no idea it was this easy." She had made a simple shift to what she was doing from the past outreaches, and she and her team saw six people say yes to Jesus. It's our job to lead people to Christ, so make sure to ask the question: "Are you ready to start a relationship with Jesus and be born again?" Then walk them through a prayer asking Jesus to forgive and save them. There is no specific sinners' prayer in the Bible, but you can lead them in a prayer from the heart. "Jesus, make me born again."

While in Brazil, I was walking down the street when I suddenly felt an overwhelming sense that I wanted to share the gospel. Nobody was on the street in front of me, so I looked to the right and down a little alley. There was a barbershop, so my friends and I walked there, and with the help of a translator, I asked the three barbers if I could take a moment to share both my testimony and the gospel with them. Two of them were already believers and excitedly said, "Yes, please" and pointed to the other guy, whose name was Nicholas. I shared my testimony and the simple gospel with him. When I asked if he wanted to say yes to Jesus and be born again, he quickly responded yes. His two coworkers celebrated at that, and we all held hands right there in the barbershop and prayed with Nicholas to be born again. Daniel, my Brazilian friend, began to disciple him for the next few months. Nicholas was hungry for the things of the Lord and was growing. Those who knew him said that he was a different person after he prayed to say yes to Jesus.

Less than two months later, Nicholas passed away from complications of his past drug problem. What if I would not have stopped and shared with him? What if all I did that day was plant and water seed? Do you see the importance of reaping the harvest? It wasn't difficult at all. His friends at the barbershop had been praying, planting, and watering that seed in his heart, and God sent me to reap where others had labored. Evangelism is easy when you understand that he is the Lord of the harvest.

God Brings the Growth

"I planted, Apollos watered, but God gave the *growth*" (1 Corinthians 3:6, emphasis added).

God gives growth to the new believer. When somebody is truly ready to follow Jesus, God does the work in their heart by the Spirit. It's so fun to watch people grow in God because the Holy Spirit is teaching them and they are responding to everything that they are learning. I have learned this the hard way with people who are not truly ready to surrender all to Jesus. I want to do the best to help them, but they really don't want to grow. I have found that it is best to invest into the ones who are growing and watch the Lord do the work in them. I make room for everybody because sometimes a person has to belong until they believe. At the same time, I no longer give a ton of energy to those who are not growing in the things of the Lord because they don't really want to change.

When Kaden was saved at the mall (see the last chapter for that story), he wrote me and asked to come to my house to get a Bible. Kaden is constantly asking questions and wanting to grow in God. This is how somebody should be when they truly come to the Lord. Seasons of difficulty will happen in every new believer's walk that we will have to help them navigate, but they are going to be growing the whole time.

I thank God that growth in a new believer is not on me; it's on God and that person.

Six Lies We Believe About Evangelism

Do you believe that evangelism is easy yet? If you're like most people that I talk to, you are probably coming around to the idea, but you are facing a few barriers that still stand between you and evangelism. I have traveled all over the world and have taught these next six points that we are going to go over to many different people. These six lies about evangelism seem to be the same six lies for most people in most nations. The devil is a liar and wants to shut down the church any way that he can. He wants to keep us silent and afraid so that we won't be the light that Jesus has called us to be to the world around us. This next section of the book will be life changing if you are honest with yourself and truly get these lies as far away from you as you possibly can. You are called to change the world for Jesus. Let's remove the lies that are stopping you.

1. Evangelism is not for me

You are actually right when you say that evangelism is not for you. This very thought keeps you from doing it because it's not for you. Evangelism is for the hundreds, if not thousands, of people in your city who are ready to be saved and come into a relationship with Jesus. You see, we have bought a lie that says "evangelism is not for me because, well, honestly, I don't like it, and I don't want to do it." Since when has Christianity been about what you want and what you like to do? Do you like loving your enemies and forgiving the person who has wronged you seventy times seven? I didn't think so.

You see, the lie that has crept into the body of Christ is that Christianity is somehow about us and not the Lord. This lie has created a weak and powerless Western church because we only do what we want to do and end up creating a god in our own image and likeness that we serve out of our own comfort and convenience. That is not the Jesus that I serve.

> Then Jesus told his disciples, "If anyone would come after me, let him deny himself and take up his cross and follow me. For whoever would save his life will lose it, but whoever loses his life for my sake will find it. For what will it profit a man if he gains the whole world and forfeits his soul? Or what shall a man give in return for his soul? For the Son of Man is going to come with his angels in the glory of his Father, and then he will repay each person according to what he has done." (Matthew 16:24–27)

You see, Christianity is about denying yourself and following Jesus. Don't allow Western culture to lie to you. Being a Christian is so much more than going to church on Sunday and trying to be a good person the rest of the week. True Christianity is being sold out for Jesus every second of the day. If you think that this section is getting a bit heavy, especially since this chapter says that evangelism is easy, then buckle up as we read this next Scripture. "For none of us lives to himself, and none of us dies to himself. For if we live, we live to the Lord, and if we die, we die to the Lord. So then, whether we live or whether we die, we are the Lord's" (Romans 14:7–8).

You see, this passage in Romans says it so clearly. This life is not ours. It's his, and he bought us at a high price, the price of his Son Jesus. So we need to make sure to do our best for him in the life that we have. We only have one shot at this, so let's give it all we've got. And that is the only way to truly live for Jesus. You see, on the other side of surrender is the Spirit-empowered life where evangelism does become easy. But you have to be willing to give Jesus a full yes with no more excuses.

2. I don't evangelize because it's not my personality

I understand that we are all different with different personalities. And the last thing that I want to do is try to make you like me. You be you. Just make sure that you share your faith. I don't want you to feel pressured to share your faith, but I do want you to feel a sense of responsibility to share your faith. Why? Because we are called to do that as believers, and some pressure and responsibility might not always be negative. It's all in your perspective. When I feel pressure, I rise up and overcome it. In the church, we have gotten soft and have an attitude of "If you want to, go. If you want to, give. If you want to, fast."

But Jesus said, "You're going to go! You're going to give! And you're going to fast!"

We have lost our grit and toughness as believers and do only what we feel comfortable doing. Listen, I love soft and compassionate messages, I really do. But I have found that soft and compassionate messages don't seem to activate people in outreach. The pastor's job is to comfort the afflicted, and the evangelist's job is to afflict the comfortable. It's okay if you feel some pressure. The question is, what are you going to do with it?

The Bible says, "I have been crucified with Christ. It is no longer I who live, but Christ who lives in me. The truth is that it's no longer you who lives anyway, it's Christ that lives in you"

(Galatians 2:20). Evangelism is easy when the Christ in you takes the driver's seat and your so-called personality takes the back seat.

While on outreach with a group of students from SLS, we were going door to door. Nakoia was in my group, and at the beginning of our outreach, she was telling me she was really quiet and not that bold when it came to outreach. I said, "Not a problem," and told her that I would lead most of the conversations.

After about an hour, she suddenly yelled "Hey!" really loudly and ran across the street and started to minister to a lady through her fence. That lady ended up coming to Belong that next week. After Nakoia was done talking to the lady, I asked her where that boldness came from. She just smiled. The Holy Spirit had released her from fear. It was amazing seeing her step out of the label she had put on herself. When you begin to get your eyes off yourself, you may find yourself shouting "Hey" and running across the street to minister to somebody.

3. I'm not a street evangelist

When people hear the word *evangelism,* they often think of street evangelism. I want to warn you a very corny dad joke is coming. I'm not trying to get you killed by having you share your faith in the middle of a street with cars driving by at 50 mph. I know that was a bad joke, but I hope that you were thinking for a moment. I'm not trying to make you a street evangelist; I'm trying to encourage you to be a Christian who shares their faith everywhere they go. If you're walking down the sidewalk, then you are a sidewalk evangelist; if you're in a coffee shop, then you're a coffee shop evangelist. If you are at the gym, then you are a witness for Jesus at the gym.

I was once in Kentucky, speaking at a friend's church. We went to the YMCA to play basketball. After we played basketball, I asked the group of six young men that we were playing if I could share with them about Jesus. They said yes and let me share. When I was done sharing, I asked who wanted to be born again, and four of them said yes to Jesus. The other two were already Christians. You just need to love Jesus where you are and share him with others.

You see, the lie that the enemy tries to sell us is that we have to be extreme and out there on the streets talking to everybody, holding a sign or megaphone, confronting people with the gospel by calling them out for their sin. That may be for a few people but not for most. That would make me uncomfortable, and I would not want to do that. Evangelism is not just for the select few bold ones that will really go for it. It's for all of us. We just need to learn to share as we go.

One day, I was in Waco visiting pastor Les Cody. We were out to lunch and asked the server if we could pray for him. He said yes and asked us to pray that he would get a dog in the next few weeks. He really wanted a dog. After we prayed that the Lord would bring him a dog, I asked him when he had a few minutes to come back to the table because I wanted to share my testimony. He came back to the table. "Go for it, man. I've got some time." I shared my testimony with him and then the gospel. I asked him if he wanted to be born again, and he said yes. We prayed for him right there, and he felt the power of the Holy Spirit come into his life. A week later, he texted us to let us know that God brought him the dog that we prayed about. This is an example of being a restaurant evangelist.

We are all called to share our faith as we go. Let's look at a Scripture in Acts that shows that all in the church were actively sharing their faith and were a real threat to the devil.

Saul was one of the witnesses, and he agreed completely with the killing of Stephen. A great wave of persecution began that day, sweeping over the church in Jerusalem; and all the believers except the apostles were scattered through the regions of Judea and Samaria. (Some devout men came and buried Stephen with great mourning.) But Saul was going everywhere to destroy the church. He went from house to house, dragging out both men and women to throw them into prison. But the believers who were scattered preached the Good News about Jesus wherever they went. Philip, for example, went to the city of Samaria and told the people there about the Messiah. (Acts 8:1–5 NLT)

Paul went house to house, dragging out both men and women to throw them in prison; that means that both men and women were sharing their faith boldly. If you only knew how much of a threat you were to the devil. He is so scared of you being activated in evangelism because then he would begin to lose ground in cities where he has had strongholds for far too long. It also says that the believers who were scattered preached the good news of Jesus wherever they went. If you're a believer of Jesus, it's your job to preach everywhere you go. I love this Scripture as well because it says that the apostles stayed in Jerusalem and all the other believers were scattered. That means that those who were going everywhere preaching were not the apostles; they were just everyday believers. If we are not careful, we fall into the mentality that sharing your faith is only for the select few super-gifted leaders, but we see in Acts 8 that every Christian shared their faith. And they did this in the face of extreme persecution as well. What changed? Well, the original call never changed. We have just changed it because it's not comfortable, and we don't want to do it.

4. I'm not gifted

So many people are sidelined from sharing their faith because of the lie that they are not gifted enough. Well, let me tell you that if you are a Christian, you have been gifted the greatest gift of all time, the gift of the Holy Spirit.

"Peter replied, 'Each of you must repent of your sins and turn to God, and be baptized in the name of Jesus Christ for the forgiveness of your sins. Then you will *receive the gift of the Holy Spirit*. This promise is to you, to your children, and to those far away—all who have been called by the Lord our God'" (Acts 2:38–39 NLT, emphasis added).

You have been called by the Lord, so you have received the promise, which is the gift of the Holy Spirit. You see, there is a big difference between natural gifting and the gift of the Holy Spirit. Some people have a natural gift to communicate or to sing a beautiful song or to lead people, and that's wonderful. But in and of itself, that can't change the world. A natural gift from God used in the right way to bring glory and honor to Jesus can absolutely change the world if the person is under the lordship of Jesus. The anointing and the Holy Spirit break the yoke.

"It shall come to pass in that day that his burden will be taken away from your shoulder, and his yoke from your neck, and the yoke will be destroyed *because of the anointing oil*" (Isaiah 10:27 NKJV, emphasis added).

When people meet me for the first time they think, *Man, Chris is really gifted. He can preach in front of people and gets words of knowledge, and when he prays for people, God moves.* And they say things like, "Chris is really gifted, but I'm not." What a lie! The enemy has used this lie to shut many people down. You weren't there when I was a kid. I couldn't read, and the thought of speaking in front of people terrified me. I did not want to talk to people about Jesus. See, this is the problem with church conferences and stages because you see the person on the stage, but you didn't see them on the backside of the mountain when God was developing them. We are all the same. We are all weak, and we all need God to anoint us with his Holy Spirit so that we can be used by God to break the yoke off people's neck.

If you're reading this and still thinking, *Well I'm not gifted like that*, I have good news for you because you are the ones with the biggest target on your back for God to use. Why, you ask? Because the Bible says that he takes the weak things in the world to confound the wise.

"But God has chosen the foolish things of the world to put to shame the wise, and God has chosen the weak things of the world to put to shame the things which are mighty; and the base things of the world and the things which are despised God has chosen, and the things which are not, to bring to nothing the things that are, that no flesh should glory in His presence." (1 Corinthians 1:27–29 NKJV)

God uses the weak and base things in the world to do his work is so that he is sure to get the credit and glory for what happens. That is why God likes to use me, a dairy farmer's son from Woodland, Washington. I was a nobody from a small town who wasn't that smart or groomed in church to be a pastor. He said, "Chris will be perfect for this job because when I work through him, people will know that he could never do this in his own strength." One day, my mom was listening to me preach. She later told me the whole time I was preaching, she was thinking, *Wow, look at what God has done with my son.* You see, my mom knows that I'm not naturally that gifted but that I have been gifted with the Holy Spirit and that I have done everything in my power to steward the gift of the Holy Spirit in my life.

I want to encourage you to break off the lie that you are not gifted and daily remind yourself that the greatest gift, the gift of the Holy Spirit, is with you.

5. I just don't like pushing my beliefs on people

Sometimes we say things that sound right but are really so wrong, e.g., I just don't like pushing my beliefs on people. That sounds right until you realize that your silence is pushing them toward hell. When was the last time that Disney+ called you and asked you permission to put woke content in your kids' favorite TV shows? They didn't! When was the last time Target called you during June and asked if it was okay with you if they turned the whole store into a LGBTQI+ world? They didn't! When is the last time that the MLB called and asked your thoughts on holding a pride night at games? They didn't!

So the world is pushing its crazy demonic agenda. By the way, they can't even rightly define what a woman is, and they say that a man can have a baby. We allow this group of people that is pushing their own demonic religion on us and our nation to keep doing so with little to no resistance as we sit silently on the sidelines, thinking that we don't want to push our beliefs on them. We need to wake up and understand that this is a spiritual battle, a battle to make you be quiet and stay quiet.

We are told that we are hateful for believing in God and his Word. We are looked at as the enemy and told to stay in our churches when, in reality, we have the right message. We are the carriers of the good news. Don't you see how this lie has shut down the church and pushed us into the corner? It's time that we rise up and shout from the rooftops that Jesus is alive! This is the good news.

> For God so loved the world, that he gave his only Son, that whoever believes in him should not perish but have

eternal life. For God did not send his Son into the world to condemn the world, but in order that the world might be saved through him. Whoever believes in him is not condemned, but whoever does not believe is condemned already, because he has not believed in the name of the only Son of God. (John 3:16–18)

I want to teach you a foundational truth when it comes to the gospel. The gospel is not this: Believe in Jesus, or you will be condemned to hell. Instead, it's this: You need to believe in Jesus so that you can come out of condemnation and be born again and have eternal life with Jesus. You see, the Scripture says whoever does not believe is condemned already. When you understand that we are preaching people out of condemnation and death into life, our message now sounds great. The world without Jesus is heading to hell, and we get to come and rescue people from that road and introduce them to Jesus. I can't think of anything more important to do. "The fruit of the righteous is a tree of life, and he who wins souls is wise" (Proverbs 11:30 NKJV).

When we understand that we have the best news in the world, then we will become very bold because we will want people to know Jesus and be born again. We will begin to share the truth in love with those around us.

One day in Florida, at Tyrone Mall, I was on an outreach with a team, training somebody how to share their faith. We were in the food court and got in line to get Philly cheesesteaks. I started a conversation with the two people in front of us, and they both said that they were Christians. I asked if my friend could share the gospel with them so she could practice. They agreed, and my friend began to share. We figured out very quickly that one of them was not a real Christian. She raised her voice and told us that you can be gay and be a Christian. I very calmly but confidently told her that you can't because of what the Bible says. She responded that she didn't believe in the full Bible. I said, "It appears that you have created a God in your own image and likeness and that God can't save you."

She got very angry and began screaming at us, so we backed off, got our sandwiches, and went and sat down. About fifteen minutes later, she came walking across the food court and pointed her finger at me and said loudly, "I want to talk to you."

I thought, *I want to run away!* When she got to our table, she began to scream at the top of her lungs, "I hate my life! Do you think I want to be this way? I want to be normal like you." Once she calmed down, I took her hands and prayed for her, and she went back over to her table. As we were leaving the food court, I made sure to stop by her table. She stood up and hugged me. Her Christian aunt who was with her said, "What should I do?"

I said very plainly, "Don't change the Word of God in order to appear nice to your niece. Be a Christian and hold the line so that when she is ready, she can come to Jesus."

You see, the world has defined love as you need to accept everybody the way that they are, and if you don't accept them, then you are not loving but actually hateful. And of course, everybody is accepted for the way that they are unless you're a conservative Christian. Then you need to change. What a lie. Love is not accepting people in their sin and letting them live and die in it. Love is a person, and his name is Jesus. Love is that Jesus came from heaven to earth to rescue us all out of our sin. Don't try to help Jesus look good by not speaking the truth in love. He doesn't need your help. He is good! You can help Jesus by being full of the Holy Spirit and speaking the truth in love. When you do that, people have the opportunity to be saved.

For whoever calls on the name of the Lord shall be saved." How then shall they call on Him in whom they have not believed? And how shall they believe in Him of whom they have not heard? And how shall they hear without a preacher? And how shall they preach unless they are sent? As it is written: "How beautiful are the feet of those who preach the gospel of peace, Who bring glad tidings of good things! (Romans 10:13–15 NKJV)

You have beautiful feet. Get out there with those feet and tell people the good news.

6. I'm just too fearful

Honestly, this last lie is the one that holds the most people back from sharing their faith, the lie of fear. The enemy wants to keep you trapped in fear because if you are fearful, then you are focused on yourself and not on others around you who need Jesus. At our church, Mercy Culture, we say, "Fear, go, Holy Spirit, come!" Say it out loud once: "Fear, go, Holy Spirit, come!" That felt good, didn't it? We have to constantly tell fear to go and invite the Holy Spirit to come so that we can be bold witnesses for Jesus.

"For God has not given us a spirit of fear, but of power and of love and of a sound mind" (2 Timothy 1:7 NKJV). The Scripture says that God has not given us a spirit of fear. So here we see that fear is a demonic spirit that tries to rob us of true power, love, and a sound mind. The Bible says, "The Spirit of God, who raised Jesus from the dead, lives in you. And just as God raised Christ Jesus from the dead, he will give life to your mortal bodies by this same Spirit living within you" (Romans 8:11 NLT).

So he has not given us a spirit of fear but has given us the same spirit that raised Christ from the dead, the Holy Spirit. Have you ever been in a time of worship and you feel the presence of God so strongly that you feel like anything is possible? I call it the Samson anointing. You feel like any problem that you have will melt away and that anything that you face will dissolve like wax. I have definitely felt that way at church, often in the presence of God. But right after this moment of incredible worship, where you told the Lord, "Here I am, send me," you find yourself at the grocery store, and you hear the Holy Spirit say, "Do you see that little old lady over there with the walker? Go tell her that I love her." The moment that you hear those words "go tell her," you freeze as fear grips you. One minute ago, you were full of life and faith, and nothing was impossible. The next minute, you are paralyzed with fear. Have you ever thought about this? Has it ever dawned on you that this is spiritual and that you are in a spiritual battle and the spirit of fear is trying to stop you from carrying out what the Lord has asked you to do?

You see, we have been so trained by fear that we think this is normal. It's not. We have been so trained by fear that when we feel it, we think, *Man, I'm just really fearful.* But that's not true. When you look inside, you will not find the spirit of fear; you will find the same spirit that raised Christ from the dead. When I sense fear, I get really excited because I know something great is about to happen. I have found that fear is an invitation to crush hell, and once you crush it, step through and rescue the person on the other side.

You see, you're not the one who is fearful; the enemy is actually the one who is fearful that you will step out and be a witness. Because of this, he sends spirits of fear to intimidate you and try to scare you out of living on mission. You are such a threat to the devil that he tries to stop you by sending agents of fear. I don't know about you, but I take that as a compliment. We will probably sense fear around us for the rest of our lives, but when we have this perspective on fear, it will no longer have any effect on us and our obedience to God.

I was in Iraq, visiting a friend and his ministry, and a supernatural door opened to our team. We were able to get into a mosque to share Jesus with many Muslims. As we were driving down the streets of Baghdad to the area of the city where the mosque was, I began to sense that spirit of fear. I asked, "How dangerous is this?" Before they responded, I said, "Wait, why don't you tell me when we leave?" The moment that we arrived and got out of the van, the fear lifted and what felt like a blanket of the presence of God wrapped around me. What God did in the mosque that day was amazing. But what God revealed to me about fear was even more amazing.

He showed me that day that he is truly with us as we go in faith to share his message with the world. He taught me that obedience in going brings a peace and comfort beyond understanding to those who step out in faith at his word. This experience brought the Scriptures that we all know so well to life—Scriptures about God being our shield, comforter, and strong tower and the Scripture that states that we are under the shadow of his wing. The key that I got from this experience is that he really is all those things. These are not just nice memory verses that we learned in grade school; they are truths of the reality of the working of the Holy Spirit in our lives. He is a tangible shield, comforter, and strong tower; you just have to get yourself into a place where you need that aspect of who God is to manifest. We can't play it safe and expect to experience that aspect of who God is.

It's time to tell fear to go and ask the Holy Spirit to come. It's time to be bold for Jesus and know that when we step out in faith, he will be there to comfort us and back us with power from on high.

Evangelism is easy if you are in the presence of God. We must get this because we have a massive harvest of souls that needs to come into the kingdom of God. We don't have a harvest problem; we have a labor problem. We have a shortage of laborers because many of our laborers are stuck behind barriers of fear and lies that are holding them back from being useful in the kingdom of God.

11

WE DON'T HAVE A HARVEST PROBLEM

While in Iraq, I was on an outreach in the city, sharing with people about Jesus one on one. Before we went out, we prayed together, asking God to lead us to the one that was ready.

Our team decided to go to a barbershop and share as we were getting haircuts. About halfway through our time in the barbershop, a man, Binan, walked in and started playing video games with some of our team members. He just started hanging out with us. When it was time for us to go, I started sharing with all those in the barbershop about Jesus. I asked them all if they would like to follow Jesus, and they all said no except for Binan. He asked if we would continue to talk to him outside.

When we got outside, he began to tell us that he works right down the road at his father's shop and was hungry and wanted lunch, but he had kept feeling this pull that he had to come to the barbershop for some reason. He kept putting it off, and when he was leaving to get lunch, he decided he had to go to the barbershop and had come instead of getting lunch. He said he now knew why: He needed to meet us and pray to be born again.

This man was brought up in a Christian home in Iraq. (He was not Muslim but was not a Christian. He was not a true follower of Jesus and had no understanding of what it meant to be saved.) The next day, we met with him for two hours and discipled him in the Word of God and prayed with him as he started his new relationship with Jesus.

I have gone out on many outreaches in Iraq and honestly, most of the one-on-one outreaches are filled with conversations where we are planting and watering seeds. In America, one-on-one conversations last anywhere from two to ten minutes because most people have a framework for the gospel. But in Iraq, most conversations on outreach last much longer: from twenty-five to forty-five minutes because the people have no grid for the real gospel. This encounter in Iraq taught me something. The harvest is ripe and ready. We just have to believe God and go out and get it, no matter where we are in the world.

A little while after this encounter with Binan in Iraq, I was in Tokyo. Tokyo is one of the most unreached cities in the world. Less than 2 percent of the population is saved.[2] So as we were flying in, I was praying. "Please let us win one person for you in this city." We didn't just lead one but led eight to the Lord in Tokyo. It was amazing. The first person that we talked to that said yes to Jesus was a young man who had traveled from Okinawa. We started a conversation with him in the park, and he was happy to talk with us. We asked him if he had ever heard the good news about Jesus Christ, and he said no. After we shared with him, he wanted to pray with us to be born again.

Every city in the world is a ripe harvest field. Don't believe the bad news that you often hear, and don't believe the negative Christians out there that say it's just so dark and people are not ready for Jesus. People are ready, and we have to be willing to do the work to bring them in. We are living in harvest season, and it's time to let down your nets for a supernatural catch.

And when he had finished speaking, he said to Simon, "Put out into the deep and let down your nets for a

---

[2] "Pray for: Japan," Operation World, February 19, 2024, https://operationworld.org/locations/japan/.

catch." And Simon answered, "Master, we toiled all night and took nothing! But at your word I will let down the nets." And when they had done this, they enclosed a large number of fish, and their nets were breaking. They signaled to their partners in the other boat to come and help them. And they came and filled both the boats, so that they began to sink. (Luke 5:4–7)

A supernatural catch is coming to your city. You just need to put down your nets at his word and he will fill them with people who are ready to be saved and discipled. Do you believe it? Are you convinced that people in your city are ready for Jesus? Yes, they are; you just have to go out and bring them in.

I was in Longview, Washington, doing outreach in the city, and we were going door to door near The Promise Church. We came to a door and knocked, and the door barely opened up. I said, "Hi, my name is Chris, and we are out today from The Promise Church, looking to pray for people and share the gospel."

From behind the door, she said, "I'm a witch."

I didn't hesitate. "Well, I just heard the Lord say that you are his daughter and he loves you." The door opened up fully, and there stood Briana. We began a conversation with her about Jesus, and she prayed right there on her front porch to be born again. That very day that she was saved, she came to Belong and two of the ladies on our team went and picked her up. She brought her witchcraft books, and they burned them in the parking lot of the church, just like the book of Acts. She kept coming to Belong and church. "And a number of those who had practiced magic arts brought their books together and burned them in the sight of all. And they counted the value of them and found it came to fifty thousand pieces of silver. So the word of the Lord continued to increase and prevail mightily" (Acts 19:19–20).

This next passage that we are going to look at from Matthew is a key to understanding that we don't have a harvest problem. We are going to look very closely at four different aspects of this text. This passage has been foundational to me when it comes to equipping others in outreach and discipleship.

And Jesus went throughout all the cities and villages, teaching in their synagogues and proclaiming the gospel of the kingdom and healing every disease and every affliction. When he saw the crowds, he had compassion for them, because they were harassed and helpless, like sheep without a shepherd. Then he said to his disciples, "The harvest is plentiful, but the laborers are few; therefore pray earnestly to the Lord of the harvest to send out laborers into his harvest." (Matthew 9:35–38)

1. He saw the crowd as they really were, "harassed and helpless."

A few years ago, I was invited to a Timbers MLS soccer game in Portland. I have never been a big soccer fan, but I have always been a big sports fan and love going to pro games with my friends to take in the experience. My friends were season ticket holders and had seats in the Timbers Army section.

The Timbers Army section is where the craziest fans sit or I should say stand because they stood for the whole game. You probably already know that Portland is known for being weird and out there, well, the Timbers Army is the weirdest and out-there people from the city of Portland crammed into one section. They fly every flag that I don't agree with and stand for everything that I'm completely against as a follower of Jesus. They have been known on multiple occasions to perform gay weddings during the quarter breaks of the game. I have already told you that they stand for almost the entire game, which is long. Not only that, they walk back and forth and chant different songs full of profanity. It was not all that enjoyable, and I was, honestly, starting to get a negative attitude with all these people. At the peak of my frustration, the voice of the Holy Spirit said, "How do you like your church?"

When I heard those words in my spirit, it shook me, and my eyes were opened to see this group of people totally differently than how I viewed them before. I saw them through the eyes of Jesus. When he saw the crowd, he saw them as harassed and helpless, and I was seeing them as harassing and annoying. From that moment forward, when the Lord spoke to me, my perspective changed. I now had the ability to see the crowd as they really were.

What do you see? What do you think as you drive through your city? Do you have eyes to see the people as God sees them, or do you see them through your eyes? My prayer is that your eyes will be open to see people the right way because these same people in the crowds in this season are going to begin to fill our churches.

Let's bring this point home. What do you see when you look at the person who supports the other political party? Can you love them from your heart and show them compassion, or do you really not like them and regularly talk badly about them? I understand that we will have differences in opinion and political preference, but we need to make sure that we see every person as God sees them. If we are not careful, we will be building walls that are keeping people out of church.

We should not be surprised that sinners sin. We should not be caught off guard that people who don't know Jesus are rude and selfish. We should not be caught off guard that people who are not born again are chasing after sin. They are sinners, and that is what sinners do. We need to have eyes to see the crowds as they really are so that we can have compassion for them instead of frustration, so that we can pray for them to be saved instead of complaining about them, and so that we can reach them instead of pushing them away.

2. When he saw the crowd, he saw a plentiful harvest.

When Jesus saw the crowd he didn't just see them as they really were; he saw people who were ready to say yes to him. I have learned that I don't know who is ready or not ready to receive Jesus. It is our job to share with people, and it's God's job to do the rest.

I have started sharing with people even when I think, *This is not going to go well.* Sometimes, they end up saying yes to Jesus. I have finally reached a place where I don't try to figure out if I think people are ready or not. I simply ask them if they are ready. Most of the time, when I am confident that they are not ready (mostly based on their outward appearance) I end up being wrong. So I have decided that because Jesus said the harvest is plentiful, I will believe that everybody is ready until they tell me otherwise.

In so many Scripture passages, I think, *Man, if I was there, I don't think that I would have thought that they were ready to have an encounter with Jesus.* Examples include the woman caught in the very act of adultery, Matthew sitting at the tax booth, Simon the zealot, or Zacchaeus the chief tax collector. But all these people encountered Jesus and were radically touched by God. Honestly, I would have thought in my natural mind, *Jesus, don't waste your time.* How many opportunities do we miss each day because we look at a person's outward appearance and think they aren't ready for Jesus? Lord, forgive us for this perspective of people. Let us see people as they really are and let us see a harvest that is ripe and ready.

One night at Belong in Texas, we were doing water baptisms. A young man was there, wearing all black with long claw rings and a dog collar around his neck. Throughout the night, I had seen him repeatedly, but kept thinking, *This young guy is clearly not ready.* After the second baptism, the power of God was in the room, and he began to feel the presence of God. He walked over to the baptism tank and said that he wanted to be baptized. I replied, "You need to be saved first." He prayed right there to be born again. He then kneeled down, took off his dog collar and his rings, stood back up, and got in the water. When he came out of the water, he was baptized in the Holy Spirit and began to speak in tongues. He came back to Belong and church week after week and was transformed. The next week, he looked like a completely different person.

I'm so thankful that the harvest is ripe and that I am not the Lord of the harvest, or I would have completely missed the moment with this young man. People are ready. My question is, are you?

3. He saw that the laborers were few.

I grew up on a farm and learned how to work at a young age. I helped with the hay bale harvest in the summer as a kid when I was just old enough to roll a hay bale over. I couldn't lift it, but I could roll it. I would work in the back of the hay truck and would roll bales down to my uncle Steve who would throw them off the truck to my uncle Jim, father David, and cousins, who were helping bring in the hay harvest. Work was a way of life, and I really enjoyed it. One of the things I loved most about hauling hay was when grandpa Donald brought the big jug of ice-cold Kool-Aid. After we unloaded a truck, we got a drink. It was the best.

While working on the farm during the summers, I got to be with my cousins and family. I made money as well, which was an added benefit. So much life happened there; you wanted to be there. I planted fields with uncle Steve, put out irrigation lines with my cousin Jimmy, fixed fences with another cousin Ben, milked cows with one of the farmhands Bobby, and learned how to drive my first tractor so I could rake the hay with grandpa Donald. Once, I popped the clutch and made that little 135 pop a wheelie. His jaw dropped when the wheels hit the ground and he realized we had not fallen off. Working is fun, especially when we do it together and with family.

Chelsea told me one time that one of the reasons that she fell in love with me was because I had fun doing whatever I was doing. I think that I learned this on the farm. If work needs to be done, then you might as well have fun doing it. One of the reasons that I'm a good evangelist is because I was a good farmer and worker before I was called to the work of the ministry. Think about it. Jesus called people who were working.

"While walking by the Sea of Galilee, he saw two brothers, Simon (who is called Peter) and Andrew his brother, casting a net into the sea, for they were fishermen. And he said to them, 'Follow me, and I will make you fishers of men.' Immediately they left their nets and followed him." (Matthew 4:18–20)

Jesus called working people because he knew that they would work hard for him. It's the same today. Jesus is looking for people who know how to get to work and get the job done, because a lot of people need to come into the kingdom. When I was working on the farm at harvest time and we needed to bring in the corn silage that we fed to the cows through winter, I had to work longer hours than normal because we had a certain window of time to harvest the crop. When I think of harvest time I think, *It's time to get to work.* There was never a time when I sat in the barn and the harvest just came into the barn by itself. In the same way, the harvest isn't walking into the church either. We have to get to work and go out into our cities and bring them in.

"As Jesus passed on from there, he saw a man called Matthew sitting at the tax booth, and he said to him, 'Follow me.'

And he rose and followed him" (Matthew 9:9). I could just see Jesus walking by Matthew at the tax collector booth, thinking, *Man, Matthew is a hard worker. He is just working hard for the wrong thing.* So he walked up to him and said, "Follow me," knowing how hard he would work for him. I love that the Scripture says the laborers are few, because I'm a laborer, and I can work for the Lord. It didn't say the superstars or celebrity Christians are few. It didn't say the apostles, prophets, pastors, teachers, or even evangelists are few. It says the workers are few.

People in your city are ready to know Jesus. But these people are not coming to your church on Sunday morning on their own. You have to go to them. A prayer meeting won't get them, a Sunday service won't get them, and a church conference on evangelism won't even get them. At a certain point, you have to actually go out and get them. It's that simple—you have to leave your comfortable churches and air-conditioned offices and actually go out and talk to people and share the gospel with them. This is what I call the work of the evangelist, when we actually go out and bring people in. We pray a lot of prayers, sing a lot of songs, and go to a lot of meetings, but honestly, as good as all those things are, we are not bringing in the lost. As of 2024, our team has gone to more than ten thousand homes in Fort Worth, and we are just getting started. We have to be willing to actually go with the gospel and get to work.

Working in the harvest field is the most fun place to be because we get to see people saved, healed, and delivered weekly. You have read countless testimonies in this book. All of those happened because I was willing to work for Jesus. Will you work for Jesus? Will you help bring in the harvest? Because we need your help, and I promise you, it will be so much fun. Many people have come and spent time with us as we work in our city for Jesus, and so many of them say that they have never been around a group of people who work so hard but also have so much fun. If you ever have an opportunity to ride in the 33rd Company van, you would see that we are just a group of friends who love to work together in our Father's fields.

"He who gathers in summer is a prudent son, but he who sleeps in harvest is a son who brings shame" (Proverbs 10:5).

"As for you, always be sober-minded, endure suffering, do the work of an evangelist, fulfill your ministry" (2 Timothy 4:5).

Paul told Timothy to do the work of the evangelist. He said, "Work because it is work". This is not rocket science; it is very simple. Please get to work, and remember, it won't be glamorous, but it will be glorious.

4. Pray earnestly to the Lord of the harvest to send out laborers.

Jesus asked us to pray this prayer. "Therefore pray earnestly to the Lord of the harvest to send out laborers into his harvest." If there were ever a prayer that we should pray, it should be one that Jesus told us we should pray. Now when it comes to prayer, we should never pray a prayer that we are not willing to answer, if we have the means to answer it.

> What good is it, my brothers, if someone says he has faith but does not have works? Can that faith save him? If a brother or sister is poorly clothed and lacking in daily food, and one of you says to them, 'Go in peace, be warmed and filled,' without giving them the things needed for the body, what good is that? So also faith by itself, if it does not have works, is dead. (James 2:14–17)

This Scripture is saying that we should not just say little religious prayers but without actually doing something to help the person if we can. When God wants to do something on earth, he does it through his people. How many times have people prayed, "Lord, send out laborers," but they are not willing to be sent themselves?

Imagine a person is praying, "Lord, send out laborers," and God says back "I have been trying to by sending you!" Another person prays, "God save my neighbor." And the Lord says back, "Well, walk across the street and share the gospel with them." Another person prays, "Lord, move the mountains," and the Lord says back, "I'm trying to move the mountains, and the biggest mountain to move is you."

I know I'm being funny, but I'm trying to make a point here. We need to be willing to be used by God. I'm writing in Fredericksburg, Texas, this week and hiding away in a cabin with Chelsea, pouring out my heart on these pages. We just took a break and went to breakfast and walked through a Pacific War museum. At breakfast, as we were waiting for our table, the Lord spoke to me about the man waiting next to me. I got a word of knowledge for him and prayed for him. At our seat, the Lord spoke to me about our server. I got a word of knowledge for her and prayed for her as well before we left the restaurant. Why does this happen so often to me? It's because when I pray to the Lord to send out laborers, I'm praying for myself first. You better believe when he hears us praying that prayer, he moves because he is seeking and saving the lost through his sons and daughters.

Ekballō

Here is another really important part to this prayer that we need to understand. When Jesus said, "send out," that phrase, *send out*, has a lot more meaning to it than what is on the surface in English. In this passage, it is the Greek word *ekballō*, which means "to cast out, drive out, to send out."[3] This is the only place in Scripture where Jesus uses the word *ekballō* when talking about evangelism. The word *ekballō* has the idea of pushing people to do something against their will. Earlier in the book, I said that a little pressure isn't necessarily bad. Sometimes it takes great outside force to get us out there.

We are to pray that the Lord would send out laborers: "Now the Greek is much more forcible. It is that he would push them forward and thrust them out; it is the same word which is used for the expulsion of a devil from a man possessed. It takes great power to drive a devil out, it will need equal power from God to drive a minister out to his work.[4]

---

[3] "Lexicon :: Strong's G1544 - *ekballō*," Blue Letter Bible, accessed January 16, 2025, https://www.blueletterBible.org/lexicon/g1544/kjv/tr/0-1/.

[4] C. H. Spurgeon, "Harvest Men Needed," Blue Letter Bible, April 18, 2001, https://www.blueletterBible.org/comm/spurgeon_charles/sermons/1127.cfm?a=938038.

Jesus knew that his followers would need a kick in the butt to get out there and share with people. That is why he used the word *ekballō*. We need to pray, "Lord, here I am. Please ekballō me into my city even though I don't really want to go. I'm asking you to *cast me out* of my comfort zone, *drive me out* of my laziness, and *send me out* to those who need to know you." What about making that your prayer every morning? That would be better than a cup of coffee.

Here are six practical steps you can take to start sharing your faith this week:

1. Ask somebody if you can pray for them.
2. Ask somebody if you can share your testimony with them.
3. Ask somebody if you could share the gospel with them.
4. Take your Bible to work and read it at lunch in the break room, on your job site, or in another place that will get people's attention.
5. Invite your friends and coworkers to church.
6. One evening, go to five houses in your neighborhood and ask to pray for them and share what Jesus has done for you.

We Need to Have Great Faith and a Servant's Heart

One day, I was working on the farm with a hired hand, fixing a barbed wire fence that needed to be patched in one place and then tightened. Once we finished the patch, we started tightening a loose section. After a few cranks on the fence stretcher, the hired hand said, "That's good enough." I still remember those words as if it were yesterday.

At that, a fire rose up in me. "We don't do good enough. Let's do it right." The fence was my father's fence, and the cows inside that fence were his cows. The hired hand was not a bad guy; he just didn't take ownership as much as I did because he didn't have the last name Donald.

The best servants are sons because they take ownership of their father's businesses. Honestly, many in leadership have lost the art of serving others because they like to be served. Many fall into this dangerous trap. People start to rise in the ranks of importance, and others begin to treat them differently and serve their every need and request. It starts small and innocent with comments like,

"Let me carry that bag for you." But then it turns into people abusing their positions to take advantage of others for their own personal gain. This disease has found its way into the body of Christ, and I have seen it firsthand in green rooms and backstage environments. It makes me sick to my stomach. As true sons and daughters of God, we need to be serving others and looking to bless those around us. We need to be like Jesus. If anybody deserved to be served, it was him, but he came to serve us and rescue us from our sin.

> Though he was God, he did not think of equality with God as something to cling to. Instead, he gave up his divine privileges; he took the humble position of a slave and was born as a human being. When he appeared in human form, he humbled himself in obedience to God and died a criminal's death on a cross." (Philippians 2:6–8 NLT)

We should all be people who want to have great faith. I'm around young ministry school students often, and there is no shortage of people who want to be used by God in great ways. It's great to want to be used by God. He wants to use us all in great ways, but we need to understand that in order to be used the way that we want to be used, we first have to serve the way that he wants us to serve. If we are going to be people of great faith, then we are going to have to be sons and daughters who know how to serve.

> The Lord answered, "If you had faith even as small as a mustard seed, you could say to this mulberry tree, 'May you be uprooted and be planted in the sea,' and it would obey you! "When a servant comes in from plowing or taking care of sheep, does his master say, 'Come in and eat with me'? No, he says, 'Prepare my meal, put on your apron, and serve me while I eat. Then you can eat later.' And does the master thank the servant for doing what he was told to do? Of course not. In the same way, when you obey me you should say, 'We are unworthy servants who have simply done our duty.'" (Luke 17:6–10 NLT)

In this parable, Jesus lays out for us that if we want to be people of great faith, then we are going to need to be people who serve and do our duty. I just love this because Jesus doesn't skip a beat. He goes right from saying, "If you have faith, you can speak to this mulberry tree, and it will move" to a story about a person who works all day and comes in the house and serves some more and isn't even told thank you for the work that he did.

These works are hard, but in this mini-parable Jesus gave us the right attitude. His pleasure before our own. His people preferred, before ourselves. His name before your own name.[5]

Will you put his pleasure before your own, his people before yourself, and his name before your name? We will have to do this in order to bring in the harvest that is ripe and ready.

I was in Fort Worth on outreach going door to door. We had gone to a street a few times already and needed to continue to go to all the doors that were in that neighborhood. A few different people on the street had told us that we needed to go to this specific house, so we made it over there and knocked on the door. The front porch smelled so bad that I could hardly handle it. We knocked again to see if anybody was home, and somebody yelled at us that they were coming. When she got to the door and opened it, the smell from the house almost knocked us over. After a minute or two of talking, she said that she needed to sit down. I had a choice to make. Either I could go in the house or say goodbye. Well, I had prayed to the Lord, "Here I am, send me," so I decided I'd better go in the house. I stood right inside the door, hoping to catch some air from outside as I talked to her.

She then said, "Please shut the door. You're letting the flies in." So I had another decision. Was I shutting myself in this house? It smelled so bad because about thirty cats were in the living room, and they were using the old wood floor, not the litter box. The smell of pee was so awful, you could taste it.

I prayed for her, and as I was getting ready to leave, a guy walked around the corner. I thought, *Well I'm here. Let's preach the gospel.* After I shared with him, he prayed to be born again. By this

---

[5] David Guzik, "Study Guide for Luke 17," Blue Letter Bible, accessed January 16, 2025, https://www.blueletterBible.org/comm/guzik_david/study-guide/luke/luke-17.cfm?a=990010.

point, my eyes were burning, and flies were biting my ankles. I then told the lady about the food bank again, and she said she couldn't drive. So I offered to buy her some food from Walmart. She wanted a specific breakfast burrito, and that took another two minutes to look up before I could leave. I smelled like that house for the next hour. It was terrible. But it's what I prayed for, and I am a son. Jesus needed somebody to take care of his daughter. Since then, we have been back on multiple occasions to give her more frozen burritos and share the love of Jesus with her.

Lost but Looking

So many people in our cities are just like this, lost but looking. And we need to be God's workforce that goes and finds them. Remember to pray for eyes to see the crowds as they really are and to pray that the Lord of the Harvest will ekballō you into the harvest field.

I was flying to Kentucky to speak at a City Quake event, and my daily Bible reading that day was Luke 15, the parable of the lost sheep, the lost coin, and the lost son. I had started my travel day early with a flight out of DFW, so I was reading my Bible on the plane. I was so impacted by the different parables that day. The Lord said to me before we landed, "We are looking for what is lost." My friend Ryan picked me up and took me to my hotel to quickly drop my luggage off before we headed to the event for the day. As we were leaving the hotel, a well-dressed woman was walking in. Like I do often, as we were walking by, I asked if I could pray for her. She said "Yes." I then asked what she needed prayer for. She took a minute to think and then said, "Pray that I find my computer. I have been looking for it for a week, and it has all my important information on it from work. I need to find it, and it has been stressing me out, not knowing where it is."

Faith rose up inside me. It may sound funny, but I just knew she was going to find that computer. I said, "It's interesting that you asked me to pray for that because on my flight to Kentucky, I read Luke 15 about the lost sheep, lost coin, and lost son. And in all those parables, they found what they were looking for. I believe after we pray, you will find what you are looking for." After we prayed and walked away I thought, *That was cool*, but didn't give it much more thought because we were off to the event. I honestly didn't think I would see this lady again.

The next day, as we were leaving our room and walking by the front desk, the lady that I had prayed for was standing there. She excitedly said, "You won't believe it. I went home and walked into my house and right to my computer. It was right there in front of me. God helped me find it." She was actually the hotel manager, which explained why she was dressed so nicely the day before. She had been telling all the hotel staff that morning what God had done for her. It made for a very easy evangelism moment with the staff.

This is such a fun testimony of what God did, but oftentimes, God does something like this to teach us a much deeper truth. Yes, that computer meant a lot to the hotel manager, just like the lost sheep and lost coin meant a lot to their owners. But the truth is God's lost kids mean a lot more to him than anything here on earth could ever mean to us. And the truth is that his kids are lost but they are looking.

> Jesus entered Jericho and made his way through the town. There was a man there named Zacchaeus. He was the chief tax collector in the region, and he had become very rich. He tried to get a look at Jesus, but he was too short to see over the crowd. So he ran ahead and climbed a sycamore-fig tree beside the road, for Jesus was going to pass that way. When Jesus came by, he looked up at Zacchaeus and called him by name. "Zacchaeus!" he said. "Quick, come down! I must be a guest in your home today." Zacchaeus quickly climbed down and took Jesus to his house in great excitement and joy. But the people were displeased. "He has gone to be the guest of a notorious sinner," they grumbled. Meanwhile, Zacchaeus stood before the Lord and said, "I will give half my wealth to the poor, Lord, and if I have cheated people on their taxes, I will give them back four times as much!" Jesus responded, "Salvation has come to this home today, for this man has shown himself to be a true son of Abraham. For the Son of Man came to seek and save those who are lost. (Luke 19:1–10 NLT)

Zacchaeus was lost, but he climbed that tree because he was looking, and Jesus came to look for the lost. Luke 19:10 says so clearly, "For the Son of Man came to seek and save those who are lost" (NLT). My question for you today is, are you looking to seek and save the lost like Jesus? Think back to a time when you lost your car keys. You looked for those until you found them, didn't you? And you really didn't care how ridiculous you looked when you were trying to find them. You just kept looking, sometimes under the same couch five times until you found them. Or think about when you misplace your cell phone or even worse, drop it in a Porta Potty and have to reach in and get it. I have a friend whose wife dropped her phone in a Porta Potty, and he counted the cost and went in after it.

We go to extreme measures to find lost items, but are we willing to go to extreme measures to rescue God's lost kids? During one of our internships, a student who was growing in compassion for people shared a revelation that had brought a great breakthrough in her life. She loved animals. One day, she was driving home, and a cat was in the middle of a busy road and didn't know what to do. Without thinking, she pulled her car over, jumped out, and ran into the road to get the cat to safety. The Lord had brought this story back to her remembrance and said, "You will risk your life for a cat. I need you to do the same for my lost children."

As we bring this chapter to a close, I hope that you have a new sense of passion to get to work in the harvest field. We don't have a harvest problem; we have a worker problem. If we can all get busy looking for the lost, then we will begin to see many who are lost but looking come to Jesus. It is time that we all begin to run the race that God has prepared for us.

12

RUN YOUR RACE

At Woodland High School, the home of the Beavers, I ran track and field. I competed in the 110-meter high hurdles, the 300 hurdles and the 4 by 1600-meter relay. One day, I was over by the long-jump pit, practicing the 300 hurdles, and the track coach and the three fastest guys on the track team walked up to me. I knew something was up, but I didn't know what. They asked if I would run the 4 by 100-meter relay race with them. "Chris, we know you're not that fast, but you can run. And you are not clumsy, so you can pass the baton off without dropping it." I didn't know whether to take what they said as an insult or compliment. I decided it was a compliment and signed up for the relay team.

In the 4 by 100-meter relay, every runner runs 100 meters as fast as they can. The first leg was the second-fastest person, the second leg was the third fastest, the third leg was the slowest (me), and the fourth leg was the fastest runner on the team. If you have ever seen track spikes, they are shoes with sharp spikes on the bottom to give you traction. When the runner was coming toward me, I was extra motivated to run faster because I didn't want to take a spike to the back of my leg. Also, the person who I passed the baton to was a lot faster than me, so I had to run as fast as I could to get the baton in his hand before we crossed over the line. If you pass that line before the baton is passed, you are disqualified.

I didn't want to be disqualified, so I ran as hard as I could and stayed in my lane.

Almost every race went something like this. We would be leading the race the first two legs. Then I would get the baton, and all the teams would catch up or even pass us. Then I would pass the baton to the anchor leg, and he would win the race because he was so fast. I just had to run my race, stay in the lane, and pass that baton off to the next runner. And the runner at the end of the race, who would win, represented me. So not only would he win the race but the entire team would win the race.

Listen, you may be reading this and feel like me on the track relay team: slow and like your life is not that significant. But I'm telling you, you need to get in the race and run. Because it doesn't matter where you finish as long as you pass that baton off to your children and grandchildren. God always saves the best for last; the fastest generation to ever run is coming. We just need to run the race before us and carry the fire to the next leg of the race.

I believe the first leg was the apostles, the second fastest to ever run this race. But a generation is coming that will be the fastest to ever run. God always saves the best for last. So my question for you is this: Do you believe that your life has significance? Do you believe that your life is as significant as Paul, David, and Esther? Well, I'm here to tell you that it is, because you are running the same race as them, and their race is not complete until we run ours. This gives me so much purpose, knowing that my life is significant and that I'm a part of something so much greater than myself. We are truly a part of the greatest story ever told, and we need to run our race to win.

"Therefore, since we are surrounded by so great a cloud of witnesses, let us also lay aside every *weight*, and *sin* which clings so closely, and let us run with endurance the race that is set before us" (Hebrews 12:1, emphasis added).

The only person that can run your race is you. It's time to lay aside every weight and sin, pick up the fire of God, and run the race before us to win it.

> Don't you realize that in a race everyone runs, but only one person gets the prize? So run to win! All athletes are disciplined in their training. They do it to win a prize that

will fade away, but we do it for an eternal prize. So I run with purpose in every step. I am not just shadowboxing. I discipline my body like an athlete, training it to do what it should. Otherwise, I fear that after preaching to others I myself might be disqualified. (1 Corinthians 9:24–27 NLT)

We are all busy; if we are honest, we are all too busy. I once thought, *If everybody is busy doing stuff, then I'm going to be busy doing the stuff that he called us to do.* I want to run this race to win. Just like a relay race, we have to run within the boundary lines of our lane. We will be disqualified if we run too far to the right or the left. We have to make sure to receive the baton before we cross a certain line and pass it off before we cross a certain line. Honestly, many Christians are not running to win the race or have found themselves crossing those lines and being disqualified. The line on the left side is weight and the line on the right side is sin. Like I said, we need to lay down weight and sin, pick up the fire, and run.

Weight

Weight is anything in our lives that slows us down from running the race in front of us with determination as quickly as we can. I won't give you a long list of behaviors that could be weights because the Holy Spirit tells each person what those are and asks you to give him what has been taking your attention away from him. Why am I so confident of this? Because he comes to me daily and helps me shed weight that needs to be removed from my life so that I run straight and fast toward the finish line and don't step out of my lane and become disqualified. Hebrews 12:2 tells us how this is possible. "Looking to Jesus, the founder and perfector of our faith, who for the joy that was set before him endured the cross, despising the shame, and is seated at the right hand of the throne of God." It says, "looking to Jesus, the founder and perfector of our faith." The only way that we will stay on course and not be disqualified is by keeping our eyes on Jesus.

Back in the day, when I would plant grass fields on the farm or rake hay into windrows in the field so the bailer could come and bale the hay, I would find an object at the end of the field to focus on so that I would keep the tractor in a straight line. If I began to look to the right or left, then I would get off course and not plant the field correctly or make it more difficult for them to bale hay. I had to keep the tractor in a straight line. It's way more important to keep your life in a straight line, which only happens when you keep your eyes on Jesus.

"Dear children, keep away from anything that might take God's place in your hearts" (1 John 5:21 NLT). Keep away from anything that draws your attention away from God. It may start out as just watching the NFL on Sunday when your team plays. But then it turns into watching three games on Sunday; then, that's not enough, so you watch Monday night football games as well. Then you get so hooked on football that you add Thursday night football to the schedule. Football is not bad. I like football and cheering on the Seahawks. But a football game, on average, is three hours and twelve minutes long. That might be fine once a week, but five times a week is a bit much, since it would be about sixteen hours of football. I know people who watch that much football a week and more. That's excessive, and that's not counting watching the NFL news and checking the ESPN app every day, who knows how many times? When you take time to think about it, football, as fun as it is, carries no weight in eternity at the end of the day. The Super Bowl winner is completely irrelevant two years from now, let alone in eternity.

We need to keep away from anything that draws our eyes off Jesus and onto the things of the world. The Lord does this by simply asking for one thing at a time. We don't need to get overwhelmed on this journey. God is a good father and knows how to parent us really well. All we need to do is respond to his little nudges. In many seasons, the Lord has come to me and taken things away to make sure that my eyes stayed on him. I'm thankful for these seasons when he prunes me and removes things that aren't even bad, but if they went unchecked, they could possibly reach an unhealthy place.

"You must worship no other gods, for the Lord, whose very name is Jealous, is a God who is jealous about his relationship with you" (Exodus 34:14 NLT). Our God is a jealous God, which is not negative at all but very positive. He—the Creator of the universe—wants to have a relationship with us. He doesn't want anything to get in the way of that relationship. So he comes to talk to us daily about areas that have the potential, if we are not careful, to get us off course. Conviction from the Holy Spirit is not negative; it's actually helpful, and we want it in our lives regularly. Conviction keeps us away from sin and running the race that is in front of us. There is no better feeling in the world than being right with God.

"The wicked flee when no one pursues, but the righteous are bold as a lion" (Proverbs 28:1).

Sin

It's so sad when people have worked so hard for something for many years and it's torn down in a moment because of a wrong choice and sin. We have all heard and seen the pastors and leaders that have fallen morally and end up hurting their families, churches, and all those who looked to them for spiritual guidance. No leader is perfect, and all are susceptible to sin. The only way to overcome sin is to keep our eyes on Jesus and live right before God every day.

As I'm writing this chapter in 2024, another major leader in the body of Christ just fell morally, and to make it even worse, this was not an isolated incident. It was a pattern of sin that had been going on for decades. This is so sad and another casualty in the body of Christ. We need to stay far away from sin that leads to destruction. When they got into ministry, none of the leaders who have fallen thought, *I'm going to fall.* In fact, they probably thought the exact opposite, *I'm not going to fall.* But somewhere down the line, they allowed the weight to turn to sin and compromised. "Temptation comes from our own desires, which entice us and drag us away. These desires give birth to sinful actions. And when sin is allowed to grow, it gives birth to death" (James 1:14–15 NLT).

We can finish well. Many have finished well before us. But we must guard our hearts and minds so that no compromise creeps in that can drag us away. That will give birth to sin, which will bring death.

The good news is that if we do sin, we have an advocate. "My little children, I am writing these things to you so that you may not sin. But if anyone does sin, we have an advocate with the Father, Jesus Christ the righteous. He is the propitiation for our sins, and not for ours only but also for the sins of the whole world" (1 John 2:1–2).

Jesus is so good that he forgives us all of our sins if we sincerely repent before God. Even so, the sin that we commit still carries consequences. In other words, if a pastor, who has been leading a church for twenty-five years, has an affair and confesses his sin to God, his wife, the elders of the church, and his congregation, then he is forgiven and made right with God. But that does not mean that he will be preaching next week as if nothing ever happened. God is loving and forgiving, yes, but the sin and deception that the pastor lived in are major issues. Due to his actions, he has been disqualified from that position as a pastor. He crossed the line and doesn't meet the qualifications of a leader in the body of Christ. He needs to go through a process of restoration to his wife, family, and God. He has not been disqualified from salvation, but he will no longer be the lead pastor.

Sin carries consequences that greatly affect our life and ministry; this is why it says "lay aside all weight and sin." Weight can turn to sin very quickly. If you're reading this and you're living in sin, I want to encourage you to reach out to a pastor at your church and do what the Bible says. "Therefore, confess your sins to one another and pray for one another, that you may be healed. The prayer of a righteous person has great power as it is working" (James 5:16).

We can get free and stay free from sin, and we need to so that we can run the race before us to win. The thing is, we are not just trying to get rid of weight and sin; we are actually picking up the fire of God and running with it so that we can pass the baton to the next generation and help change the world. We are laying down weight and sin, yes, but we are picking up something far better than we are putting down.

A Great Cloud of Witnesses

We are surrounded by a great cloud of witnesses that is cheering us on. Right now, Peter is walking over to Paul in heaven and saying, "Hey, they are reading that chapter in Chris's book where he tries to convince them that they are running the same race we did. You know, where he is trying to get them to see that their life has real significance. I hope they get it because our race is not complete until theirs is." Do you see it? Do you have a new excitement about life? Are you ready to live with your mission being where your feet are?

You must understand that you are a part of something so much bigger than what you think. Think about it one more time; the God of Abraham, Issac, and Jacob is your God, and you are on that timeline. Not only are you on the timeline, but you are a key player in what God wants to do on earth. Let's zoom out once more and show you the grand scale of what we are a part of. The prophets prophesied it, Jesus came and proclaimed it, the apostles ran with it, and we are called to advance it.

The Prophets Prophesied

> For to us a child is born, to us a son is given; and the government shall be upon his shoulder, and his name shall be called Wonderful Counselor, Mighty God, Everlasting Father, Prince of Peace. Of the increase of his government and of peace there will be no end, on the throne of David and over his kingdom, to establish it and to uphold it with justice and with righteousness from this time forth and forevermore. The zeal of the Lord of hosts will do this (Isaiah 9:6–7).

"The Spirit of the Lord God is upon me, because the Lord has anointed me to bring good news to the poor; he has sent me to bind up the brokenhearted, to proclaim liberty to the captives, and the opening of the prison to those who are bound; to proclaim the year of the Lord's favor" (Isaiah 61:1–2).

The prophets prophesied the coming of Jesus and what he would do for us when he came. Jesus fulfilled more than three hundred prophecies from the Old Testament spoken by the prophets.

Jesus Proclaimed It

> And he came to Nazareth, where he had been brought up. And as was his custom, he went to the synagogue on the Sabbath day, and he stood up to read. And the scroll of the prophet Isaiah was given to him. He unrolled the scroll and found the place where it was written, "The Spirit of the Lord is upon me, because he has anointed me to proclaim good news to the poor. He has sent me to proclaim liberty to the captives and recovering of sight to the blind, to set at liberty those who are oppressed, to proclaim the year of the Lord's favor." And he rolled up the scroll and gave it back to the attendant and sat down. And the eyes of all in the synagogue were fixed on him. And he began to say to them, "Today this Scripture has been fulfilled in your hearing." And all spoke well of him and marveled at the gracious words that were coming from his mouth. And they said, "Is not this Joseph's son?" (Luke 4:16–22).

When Jesus came, he did not shy away from telling people who he was. He boldly proclaimed that he came to fulfill what the prophets had prophesied. The book of John records the seven "I am" statements of Jesus.

- I am the bread of life. John 6:35, 48, 51
- I am the light of the world. John 8:12; 9:5
- I am the door of the sheep. John 10:7, 9
- I am the good shepherd. John 10:11, 14
- I am the resurrection and the life. John 11:25
- I am the way, the truth, and the life. John 14:6
- I am the true vine. John 15:1

Jesus told the world who he was and didn't just talk about it but performed miracles, forgave people's sin, died on the cross for you and me, and rose again on the third day. Jesus is God!

Just like the prophets foretold, Jesus prophesied to his followers before he ascended into heaven that he was going to send the Holy Spirit. He told them to go and wait for the Spirit to come before they began to make disciples. This prophecy happened fifty days after he prophesied it on the day of Pentecost.

> When the day of Pentecost arrived, they were all together in one place. And suddenly there came from heaven a sound like a mighty rushing wind, and it filled the entire house where they were sitting. And divided tongues as of fire appeared to them and rested on each one of them. And they were all filled with the Holy Spirit and began to speak in other tongues as the Spirit gave them utterance. (Acts 2:1–4)

He not only prophesied that the Holy Spirit would come but also prophesied that he would come back one day for a pure and spotless bride. We know this will happen because he sent the Holy Spirit as a sign that he is a true prophet. If he fulfilled one prophecy, he will, without a doubt, fulfill the second that he is coming back soon.

"Let not your hearts be troubled. Believe in God; believe also in me. In my Father's house are many rooms. If it were not so, would I have told you that I go to prepare a place for you? And if I go and prepare a place for you, I will come again and will take you to myself, that where I am you may be also" (John 14:1–3).

The Apostles Ran with It

The moment that the Holy Spirit fell on the apostles, they took off running and didn't look back. "But Peter said, 'I have no silver and gold, but what I do have I give to you. In the name of Jesus Christ of Nazareth, rise up and walk!' And he took him by the right hand and raised him up, and immediately his feet and ankles were made strong" (Acts 3:6–7). They believed Jesus at his word and didn't doubt that the Holy Spirit was with them. That is evident in stories like Acts 3 at the gate called Beautiful. They truly ran their races well and passed the baton off to the future generations that would run after them. It's amazing what these men accomplished with the Holy Spirit. They truly turned the world upside down and made a way for us to continue. All of them finished well, except for Judas, who betrayed the Lord. The apostles were great individuals who God used to start what would become known as The Way and then eventually known as Christianity. It has spread around the world and is the largest religion today. I'm so thankful for our apostolic fathers who went before us.

We Continue to Advance with It

It's now our job to continue to advance what the prophets prophesied, what Jesus proclaimed, and what the apostle ran with. In Acts 5, we read an incredible story. The apostles were performing many signs and wonders among the people, and a high priest and his officials, who were Sadducees, got jealous because the people were paying more attention to the apostles than them. So they arrested them. That night, an angel came, broke them out of prison, and told them to go back to the temple the next morning and continue teaching. When the leaders look for them the next day, they are not in prison but back in the temple. Let's pick up the story here.

> And when they had brought them, they set them before the council. And the high priest questioned them, saying, "We strictly charged you not to teach in this name, yet here you have filled Jerusalem with your teaching, and you intend to bring this man's blood upon us." But Peter and the apostles answered, "We must obey God rather than men. The God of our fathers raised Jesus, whom you killed by hanging him on a tree. God exalted him at his right hand as Leader and Savior, to give repentance to Israel and forgiveness of sins. And we are witnesses to these things, and so is the Holy Spirit, whom God has given to those who obey him." When they heard this, they were enraged and wanted to kill them. But a Pharisee in the council named Gamaliel, a teacher of the law held in honor by all the people, stood up and gave orders to put the men outside for a little while. And he said to them, "Men of Israel, take care what you are about to do with these men. For before these days Theudas

rose up, claiming to be somebody, and a number of men, about four hundred, joined him. He was killed, and all who followed him were dispersed and came to nothing. After him Judas the Galilean rose up in the days of the census and drew away some of the people after him. He too perished, and all who followed him were scattered. So in the present case I tell you, keep away from these men and let them alone, for if this plan or this undertaking is of man, it will fail; but if it is of God, you will not be able to overthrow them. You might even be found opposing God!" So they took his advice." (Acts 5:27–39)

Gamaliel said to let them be because if this was not of God, then it would come to nothing, but if it was of God, then they would not be able to stop it. Well, here we are two thousand years later, and we are preaching the same gospel that they preached in the same name that they preached, Jesus Christ of Nazareth. Do you see it? We are a part of the same story. Even though many people throughout history tried to snuff out and destroy the church, they have not been successful because this is the work of God and nothing can stand against him and his Word. We have a part to play in moving the kingdom forward.

After you have read this chapter, I hope you are ready to partner with God to do great exploits for him. We are running an exciting race that is full of surprises along the way, and there is no better way to live than to fulfill what he put you here on earth to do.

13

PARTNER WITH GOD

In this last chapter, I will share a key that the Lord gave me that truly changed my life when it comes to partnering with God. This whole book is about partnering with God to bring heaven to earth in your life and to those around you. We are called to change the world with Jesus, and when we live this way, it's so fulfilling and fun. The Lord desires to partner with us and uses situations as an opportunity to test us. Now if you are like me, I never liked being tested because I was not a very good test taker, and tests revealed what I didn't know, which happened to be a lot, especially in middle school and high school. But when the Lord tests us, it's not to reveal what we can do or what we know; the test is actually designed to reveal what he can do and what he knows. So really, the test comes down to if we can trust Jesus.

The Test that Brought the Key

At the beginning of 2023, the Lord began to open big doors for our ministry, 33rd Company. I was on a call with one of my friends, David John Philips, pastor of Real Church in Clearwater, Florida, who is also a part of the 33rd Company. He was excited that a Jesus festival that we were planning in Pakistan would actually be much bigger than we initially thought; attendance was originally estimated at thirty thousand people but had now grown to fifty thousand people. I initially was smiling, but when the call ended, my shoulders slumped as if a huge weight were set on them. I thought, *We have the budget for the thirty-thousand-person event but not for the fifty-thousand-person event.* The difference in the amount of money needed was huge.

During this time, other pressures in both life and ministry were beginning to weigh on me. In practical terms, I was a father of four growing children and wanted to be a good husband that served his wife like Jesus served the church. That was hard enough. Pressures in life can just come and go like the weather.

One night, while on a trip, I called Chelsea before she put the kids to bed. As we were talking about what we were facing, we both agreed that it may just be better to stop what we were doing and live a normal nine-to-five life and stop thinking that we could change the world. I said, "If that is what you want, I have no problem stopping tomorrow." I was really in a place where I would have been okay stopping. Ministry was not what I wanted to do but what I was called to, so it has never been my identity. I am just as happy at home on the couch as I am on a plane flying to Tokyo.

(By the way, I'm writing this final chapter while flying to Tokyo.) After we talked, we decided to pray and just see what the Lord said in the next few days. We both felt that we wanted to give up because, to be honest, it wasn't easy. Life is difficult enough just trying to navigate it, let alone trying to change the world with Jesus every day.

You see, we were being tested. Thank God, the Lord doesn't give us pop quizzes because if he would have given me a pop quiz after the phone call with David about Pakistan or Chelsea, I would have failed the test. The Lord tests us over a period of time, and the test is to reveal what the Lord can do, not what you can do. My pastor, Landon Schott, says that we are tested for two reasons: to see if it is about us and to see if we will give up. I was being tested, and the Lord was checking to see if it was about me and if I would give up.

The next morning, Chelsea woke up, got her coffee, and sat down in the front room of the house. Noah, my five-year-old, and Esther, my three-year-old, were playing on the floor. Noah had one of Ellie's worship flags that she used for dancing. As he sat there, out of nowhere, he began to sing a song that he had never sang before or since. "Never gonna give up, never gonna give up, do it, do it, do it!" Chelsea recorded it on her phone without him knowing. She sent it to me with a crying face emoji and said, "We are never going to give up." The Holy Spirit spoke powerfully through our son. And it reminded us that it's not about us but about him and what he has called us to do.

As we got closer to the deadline for needing the funds for the Pakistan trip, the pressure on my shoulders mounted. I began to go on prayer walks that were, honestly, much more complain-to-the-Lord walks. My perspective needed a readjustment. This blessing seemed to be more of a weight and a problem. Yes, the Lord wanted to partner with me, but I was honestly failing the test miserably. But I love how patient the Lord is and that he is a good teacher who allows us to feel the weight, knowing that it will pull us deeper into him and his strength.

I knew from the beginning of my walk with the Lord that he wants to partner with us in the little things, but I forgot that the Scripture says that being faithful in the little will lead to bigger things. "If you are faithful in little things, you will be faithful in large ones. But if you are dishonest in little things, you won't be honest with greater responsibilities" (Luke 16:10 NLT).

A person is faithful to steward the little because a good steward sees nothing as little. A good steward stewards the one person in front of them at the mall that needs to hear the gospel as well as they would steward fifty thousand people in front of them in Pakistan. Over my life, I have stewarded the little things with Jesus. I read the Bible and encounter the Lord daily. I witnessed to the people that I was around daily and saw people healed, saved, and delivered. I was a good steward with the little.

Here is an example of this. One day, I was speaking at a youth camp in Oregon. After I was done preaching, we walked into the lodge where we were staying, and a cleaning lady was walking down the hallway. I began a conversation with her but could tell she was not interested in talking to me. She said, "I'm a Wiccan, and I don't like the church."

I immediately got three words of knowledge for her, and they were all exactly right on. She was shocked that I knew this and asked me how I knew. I explained it was by the Holy Spirit. These words of knowledge then opened the door for me to begin to share the gospel with her. After a short conversation, she prayed with me to be truly born again.

I'm big on discipleship, so I asked her where she lived so I could help her connect with a church in her area. To my great surprise, she said, "I'm building a tiny home and live in LaCenter at the moment." LaCenter was only ten minutes away from Woodland where The Promise Church is located. We exchanged numbers, and Pastor Jonathan began to bring church members over to help her finish her tiny home. It was amazing to see what the Lord began to do.

At that time, I was moving to Texas, so when I came back home to visit a few months later, I had the opportunity to see the tiny home that the church helped finish and also had the awesome opportunity to baptize her at church on a Sunday morning. I say this with all humility, but this is a small thing, and testimonies like this happen to me weekly as I walk out what the Lord has for me to do.

The Lord had seen my faithfulness with the little things over the years, and now he was asking me to be faithful with something bigger. The Lord sees your faithfulness in the small things and your everyday steps of simple obedience. He had watched me care for the one over and over again and thought, *Okay, Chris is ready for something bigger.* The bigger thing that God was calling me to do was much bigger than what I had ever believed for up to that point, and it was a big stretching process as God was growing me. God is totally into the process of making you a son or daughter that believes him for great things. He loves stretching you and knows you can deal with the pressure if that calls you into greater things.

When I was in the middle of this pressing season, my daily Bible reading was in John 6. I have historically heard God in times of growth and pressing through the written Word of God. In many similar seasons, God spoke to me directly from the Word, which was the key to my breakthrough and understanding what God was trying to teach me. The Word of God is alive, and if you need an encounter with the Lord, read his beautiful Word.

As I was reading John 6 about the feeding of the five thousand that day, the Holy Spirit was almost shouting at me. "This is the answer that you are looking for. This is the key that the

Lord is trying to put in your hand in this season." My heart was moved, and the Spirit of God began to speak to me about the simple truth that God wants to partner with me in the small and the big. Think about that for a moment. God, the creator of heaven and earth, wants to partner with me. Are you kidding me? It's absolutely wild that God knows me and wants to invite me in on what he is doing on the earth and with the human race.

Please take a moment to read John 6:1–14. (See the next paragraph.) I read a lot of books, and I understand it can be a real struggle to slow down while reading and actually focus on the Scripture and take it in. Please take your time to read this passage. Before you read it, please pray that the Lord will open your eyes to see the wonderful revelation that God wants to partner with you. And hear me for a moment. I'm talking to you, not your pastor that preaches on Sunday morning or the person that you sit by in church that is super bold or the person that has a wild testimony. I'm talking to you. God wants to partner with *you* to change the world. And how do you do that? You simply change the world around you, live in obedience to God, and say yes to whatever he asks you to do. After you read through this Scripture prayerfully, we will review four points.

> After this Jesus went away to the other side of the Sea of Galilee, which is the Sea of Tiberias. And a large crowd was following him, because they saw the signs that he was doing on the sick. Jesus went up on the mountain, and there he sat down with his disciples. Now the Passover, the feast of the Jews, was at hand. Lifting up his eyes, then, and seeing that a large crowd was coming toward him, *Jesus said to Philip, "Where are we to buy bread, so that these people may eat?" He said this to test him, for he himself knew what he would do. Philip answered him, "Two hundred denarii worth of bread would not be enough for each of them to get a little." One of his disciples, Andrew, Simon Peter's brother, said to him, "There is a boy here who has five barley loaves and two fish, but what are they for so many?"* Jesus said, "Have the people sit down." Now there was much grass in the place. So the men sat down, about five thousand in number. Jesus then took the loaves, and when he had

given thanks, he distributed them to those who were seated. So also the fish, as much as they wanted. And when they had eaten their fill, he told his disciples, "Gather up the leftover fragments, that nothing may be lost." So they gathered them up and filled twelve baskets with fragments from the five barley loaves left by those who had eaten. When the people saw the sign that he had done, they said, "This is indeed the Prophet who is to come into the world!" (John 6:1–14, emphasis added)

God Wants to Partner with You

God wants to partner with you. Do you believe it yet? It's so easy to sit in church and think, *I know that God wants to use that person, but does he really want to use me?* I'm here to tell you that he does. Remember, the harvest is ripe, but the workers are few. God needs workers that are willing to partner with him in small and big matters to see his kingdom come and his will be done on earth.

The above passage tells us, "Jesus said to Philip, 'Where are we to buy bread, so that these people may eat?'" Here, God is asking Philip to partner with him in solving this problem. What was the problem? A lot of people needed to be fed, and the food was not on hand. The money was not in the bank to pull that off either, and even if they did have the money, where would they find enough bread to buy to serve the people?

What was the problem that we were facing in Pakistan? God had opened up a door to share the gospel with fifty thousand people, but we only had enough money in the budget set aside for an event with thirty thousand people. Jesus was inviting us into an amazing partnership, but I was not seeing this opportunity as a blessing; it had become a burden because I was looking at the numbers in terms of what we had, not with eyes of faith. I had the wrong perspective. David and Aaron, in this process, did not waver in their faith. They stayed strong and believed. While on the outside I may have appeared strong, on the inside, I was being tested. Would I trust God and rejoice in the fact that he was asking me to partner with him in seeing a miracle?

If we're not careful, we can turn God's blessing into a burden because we don't have the right perspective and discipline needed to pull off what God is asking us to do. For a season in my early thirties, when people asked me how I was doing, I would say "I'm so tired" or "I'm so busy." A friend once replied, "You're always so tired and busy."

God used his words to bring a perspective shift to my life. I was complaining about the blessing of more responsibility because I was busy and should have been thanking God for the opportunity to partner with him in more areas because he was growing my capacity. I always said I was tired because I lacked the leadership ability to say no when I needed to and yes to the most important matters. As I have grown over the past couple of years, I no longer say that I'm so busy and complain. I also try my best to be more disciplined so that I don't get tired, and taking a true sabbath helps with that.

God wants to partner with us and give us more responsibility in his kingdom. Think about it: When God gives you more to do, he is blessing you with more ways to partner with him. Let's ask God to expand our borders and increase our capacities.

It's a Test

I knew theologically and in theory that God could provide, but when my faith was tested, I was really believing God for what I could do in my own strength with a little bit of his help and not believing for the impossible. I began to understand on a completely different level that God tests us not to see what we can do and to see what we are made of, but the test is designed to bring us to the end of ourselves so that we can see what God is made of. Every test the Lord takes me through, he gives me a key.

James 1:2–4 is absolutely true. It's not just a nice Scripture that we read when we go through a trial or face a challenge. This passage holds truth that I don't want you to miss. "Count it all joy, my brothers, when you meet trials of various kinds, for you know that the testing of your faith produces steadfastness. And let steadfastness have its full effect, that you may be perfect and complete, lacking in nothing" (James 1:2–4).

Trials and challenges in life mature and complete your faith. When you face a trial beyond what you can handle or fix in your own ability, it makes room for God to come and be God. I have come to a place where I more easily welcome trials because I have seen the faithfulness of God over and over again. He has never let me down, and every challenge that I have ever gone through has made my relationship with the Lord stronger. Anymore, when I see a trial, I walk up to it and hug it, knowing that the Lord will use that trial to make me more like him and to show me just how good and powerful he is. James says, count it joy when you face trials in your life. That's a bold statement. But I have seen that what has matured me most is the trials and tests that I have walked through. I actually find myself thanking God for allowing me to go through them.

Noah, age five, will have to mature, and the only way he is going to do that is by going through different trials and tests. I will do my best to set him up for success and will always be there for him, but I can't insulate him from the world. He will face real challenges. Each challenge will mature him and give him the opportunity to grow. God the Father knows the same is true about us. He allows us to face problems that will mature us, cause us to grow, and press into his Word and truth all the more. He is always there for us and wants us to come to him, but he understands that we will mature as we face real challenges. In this season, I was facing challenges and pressures, but the Lord knew I could handle it and that it would make me stronger and ultimately fortify my faith in him.

I hope that you can look at life's tests and what he invites you into as an opportunity to partner with God and grow in your spiritual walk with the Lord and not as a burden or weight. The Lord wants to make you more like him, and his process to do that is to allow you to face real issues so that you then grow deep in God.

Through these tests and pressures, you come to the end of ourselves, whether that test is an unpaid bill or the Lord opening up a nation to you. You always have the opportunity to encounter God in the midst of what you're going through. In Pakistan, the test was a wonderful opportunity beyond me, and in this test, the Lord gave me an amazing kingdom key when I finally surrendered my ability to him.

The Key

The passage goes on to say, "He said this to test him, for he himself knew what he would do." Do you see it? He already knew what he would do. When I read this, a light bulb came on in my head. I was struck with the revelation that Jesus already knew what he would do. The weight of what we were believing for in Pakistan lifted off me, and I just simply started thanking God that he already had a plan to make it happen.

Jesus didn't need Philip's help, but he wanted to work with Philip to feed the people. Jesus didn't need Philip's wisdom or insight; he already knew what he would do. He simply wanted Philip to be a part of his plan. How amazing is it that the Lord wanted Philip to be a part of this wonderful testimony and moment recorded in Bible history.

I was overwhelmed with the fact that Jesus already knew what he would do in Pakistan but that he wanted David, Aaron, and I to be a part of it. What an amazing honor the Lord asks us, of all people. All of a sudden, the burden became a joy. The long, complaining prayer walks turned into times of worshiping and thanking God for the privilege of partnering with him.

You see, when the Lord asked Philip how they should feed all these people, Philip answered with an impressive mathematical equation. Instead, he should have said, "I have no clue how we are going to do this, but I do know that you are God, and I'm just going to worship and thank you for even inviting me into the conversation." The key that the Lord gave me that day has changed my entire perspective on life and ministry. He already knows what he will do in every situation. All we have to do is worship and thank him for being with us and including us in his plans. Can you see it? He is God and wants to bring you into an amazing relationship to show you who he is and to mature you as a son or daughter of God.

The test was, would Philip simply give Jesus his yes? Jesus asks us the same question: Will we simply say yes to him? I want to always say yes to the Lord when he wants to partner with me.

Your Response

I want to make this very personal. What will your response to God be? He wants to partner with all of us—not just the pastors, leaders, and gifted individuals—but everybody. I'm talking to the stay-at-home moms, the construction-working fathers, and the grandparents who will read this book. You are included in partnership with God. You may never travel to Pakistan or the nations. You may simply share Jesus at the gas pump when you feel completely unqualified to do so. Or maybe you can take cookies to your neighbor across the street and ask them if you can pray for them. Remember, it starts small, and as we steward the small things, he entrusts us with bigger things. Let's look at the different responses in this story.

Philip: "Philip answered him, 'Two hundred denarii worth of bread would not be enough for each of them to get a little.'"

Philip had a great understanding of what was needed to feed the crowd, and he understood that he had two major problems: It would take more money than they had to buy all the food needed, and even if they had the money, they had nowhere to buy the food. He had a money problem, and he had a supply problem. Two hundred denarii was six months' wages, was a lot of money. When he was doing his estimation, he was budgeting just a little food. In our own human strength, we always think small where God thinks big. Philip's knowledge of the situation was accurate and quite impressive but didn't help solve the problem that they were facing. Philip thought in terms of how much money was needed to accomplish what God asked him to do. We often do the same thing: look at what we have and then try to figure out how we can do something for God in the smallest way possible. God is thinking very differently and has a completely different approach that will provide in a big way. He is a more-than-enough God.

How many times have you and I limited God in this way? He calls you to do something, but you instantly try to figure it out in terms of money and resources, and you forget that you are working with the God of miracles with no limits. If you find yourself responding this way, you must renew your mind and believe in God for great things. You are not limited if you have Jesus.

Andrew: "Andrew, Simon Peter's brother, said to him, 'There is a boy here who has five barley loaves and two fish, but what are they for so many?'"

Here, we see Andrew introducing the boy to Jesus. This is wonderful, but we see that Andrew still has doubt because he asks, "What are they for so many?" Andrew was ultimately not who God used to work the miracle—he used the boy. I hope that you want to be who God uses in the story being told on the earth today. Andrew was there to be a part of what happened, but the boy gave the Lord what he had to work a miracle. I'm using a bit of a prophetic license here with this text, but the Holy Spirit shared the following with me when I read this passage.

If we are not careful, we will always expect Jesus to use others and not us. Jesus doesn't want you to introduce somebody else to him that he could potentially use for his purpose; he wants to use you. He will use the other person as well. There is enough work to go around, and Jesus really wants to work with you, so that he can be with you and so that your faith will grow and become complete.

The boy: "There is a boy [a little boy] here who has five barley loaves and two fish."[6]

The boy freely gave what he had. He didn't have much, but what he did have, he put into the hands of God. Something small can become very big, very fast, in the hands of God. You see, God doesn't need our help but will often wait until he has our help to act. The boy had two fish, probably salted little fish, and he had five barley loaves, which were regarded as simple food, more often fit for animals or the poor than for the common people. So this little poor boy had two sardines and five loaves of Wonder bread. But look at what God accomplished with what he had been given.

We are all like this little boy. What we have to offer God is small in comparison to the need in the world, but if we put our lives into his hands, he can work miracles with our surrender and obedience. I pray that we will respond like the little boy in this account of the feeding of the five thousand. God wants to partner

---

[6] David Guzik, "Study Guide for John 6," Blue Letter Bible, accessed January 16, 2025, https://www.blueletterBible.org/comm/guzik_david/study-guide/john/john-6.cfm?a=1003001.

with us; we just have to give him what we have, and he will do the rest.

After the Lord spoke to me and told me that he already knew what he was going to do in Pakistan and that he just wanted to include me in the process, the weight lifted and joy came. I became so overwhelmed with the thought that he wanted to partner with me that I just started to worship the Lord and began thanking him for including me. As we drew closer to the date that we needed the funds for Pakistan, gifts started to come in. One church that I was preaching at one Sunday heard about the event in Pakistan and sowed ten thousand dollars into it. All the money came in when we needed it, and we actually had more than enough, so we ended up digging twenty water wells with the extra funds. Forty-seven thousand people showed up to hear the gospel, and God healed and saved many that night.

What I love most about telling this testimony is that God gets the glory. We couldn't have made the Pakistan trip happen with our own strength and resources. God opened the right doors and provided all that we needed to make it possible. When I tell the story of what God did with our obedience and our yes, people are not impressed with what we did; they are amazed at what God did and continues to do in that nation. If we are going to bring God glory, then we are going to have to believe God for what we could never do in our own strength. We must understand this as we partner with God. We need to dream big and give God our yes so that he will ultimately get the glory. This brings us to the response of the last group.

The people: "When the people saw the sign that he had done, they said, 'This is indeed the Prophet who is to come into the world!'"

When the people saw what happened through the boy's surrender of what he had, they gave God glory because they knew that only he could have done this. We are called to be just like this boy who caused people to proclaim only God could do this. Simply say yes to God and watch what he will do with your life.

The Conclusion: Just As

We have come to the end of our time together here. I'm so thankful that you have read this and invested time in learning about evangelism and discipleship. The original call never changed, and you have been called by God to be a part of the solution to the world's great need for the gospel. I want to end with one last thought from the book of John that will launch you into the world as a bold witness for Jesus. Jesus said, "Just as you sent me into the world, I am sending them into the world" (John 17:18 NLT). "Just as." What a statement Jesus made as he was praying for his disciples. Think about this for a moment. "Just as you sent me into the world, I am sending them into the world." How was Jesus sent into the world?

"For this is how God loved the world: He gave his one and only Son, so that everyone who believes in him will not perish but have eternal life. God sent his Son into the world not to judge the world, but to save the world through him" (John 3:16–17 NLT) Jesus came into the world to save the world by giving his life up for them on the cross. He came to save us from our sins. We are now sent out into the world to proclaim the good news of Jesus that saves people from their sins, to call people to repentance and salvation. We carry the message of the gospel that has the power to transform the lives of those who hear it. What a responsibility we have as ambassadors of heaven, making known what is available to mankind through Jesus. People who won't know the good news if we don't tell them.

What was his purpose in coming into the world? "For the Son of Man came to seek and save those who are lost" (Luke 19:10 NLT). Jesus came to the world to seek and save the lost. So if we are sent out just as Jesus, then some aspect of our lives will be reaching out to seek and save the lost world around us. Somewhere along the way, sharing our faith and making disciples has become optional. But I'm here to tell you, it's not optional; it's actually what you are called to do and be as a follower of Jesus.

So as we close, please listen one last time. "Just as you sent me into the world, I am sending them into the world."

The baton is in your hands! Now go and change the world one person at a time.

// TAKE ACTION

Now that we have removed the lies, barriers, and excuses that held you back from living on mission, you are probably asking, *How do I practically get started in this new lifestyle?* It's one thing to have your heart moved but another thing altogether to take action in response. I am convinced that once you get started, you will see how easy it is and will continue moving forward.

Please don't move on to the next book or topic until you have this lifestyle activated in your daily life. It's not going to be comfortable at first when you step out, but I promise you that you will experience the grace and empowerment of the Holy Spirit as you go. Remember you must *go* in order to grow.

The following is a list of ways you can get started today:

Learn and Practice the Gospel Guide

The Gospel Guide, included in the back of the book, will help you get started in sharing your faith. Many people struggle to start a gospel conversation. In most cases, however, deep down, believers know the gospel. They often just fail to keep it simple and easy to understand. We don't need to start in Genesis and end in Revelation when sharing the gospel. The Gospel Guide will get you started and help you present the gospel clearly until it begins to flow naturally from your heart.

Whether it is the lyrics to your favorite song, the recipe to your favorite dessert, or the roster of your favorite sports team, we all have the ability as humans to learn, memorize, and share with others what we set our heart on. Will you set your heart on being able to clearly and concisely share the gospel? I'm asking you to learn how to do this using the two questions and gospel statement. Maybe even consider taking a break from social media until you have the Gospel Guide memorized so that you will be ready to share the gospel when the Holy Spirit prompts you.

The Gospel Guide is not meant to be a tract you hand out or something you carry with you. It is simply a tool, like a GPS system, that gets you heading in the right direction until you know the way yourself. You will be surprised how easy it is and how having a road map can create space for the Holy Spirit to lead you. For an expanded look at using the Gospel Guide or to print additional copies for your friends, family, and fellow laborers, scan the QR code on the included guide.

Ask Others if They Have Been Born Again

Also included in the back of the book is a little card that has helped our teams lead many individuals to the Lord. On the front is a simple question, "Have You Been Born Again?" and on the back is John 3:1–6 in the NLT. I always carry these cards with me and often ask people if they have been born again. Typically, they reply, "No, I have never heard what it means to be born again." You will be surprised how many individuals who attend church have not heard what it means to be born again. I then ask them if they would be okay with me reading to them six verses from John chapter three. Most of the time, the answer is "yes." As I read the six verses, I often emphasize how we were all born wrong, born in sin, and how we need to be born again, to be born right, born of God. Once finished, I ask them if they would like to be born again. It's truly that simple. Kaden, Madison, Eric, Phil, Gaige, Carlos, and many others gave their life to Jesus because I asked them this simple question.

Even if a person's initial answer is "yes, I know what it means to be born again," I always ask them to explain it to me. In many cases, the person's idea of being born again is wrong and not one bit biblical. I take the opportunity, then, to share with them what Jesus says it means to be born again and how they can enter into a relationship with him.

This is such an easy way to share the gospel in environments where many profess to be believers or to go to church. Going to church doesn't save someone—Jesus does. Get familiar with John chapter three, be bold and ask people if they have been born again. Even without the included card, you can ask people this question and use the Bible app on your phone as a reference for John 3:1–6. If you would like additional instruction on sharing the gospel with John chapter three, check out the video titled John 3:1–6 on 33rd Company's YouTube channel (@thirtythirdcompany)

Share Jesus with One Person a Day

What if you talked with one person about Jesus every day for an entire year? By the end of the year, you would have had at least 365 conversations about Jesus. That would be amazing! Practically, this could look like:

- telling someone that Jesus loves them,
- asking if you could share the gospel with them,
- seeing if there is anything you could pray for,
- asking if they have been born again,
- or a beautiful combination of the above.

Why not start today? Put a note on your bathroom mirror, refrigerator, or car dashboard. Make it your wallpaper on your cell phone. Add a recurring reminder on your phone to share with one person when you are on lunch break. Add it to your daily to-do list. Each of these steps are easy and will help remind you to take action until sharing your faith becomes a part of your everyday life. Stop making excuses, step out, and just watch what simple obedience will do. If you miss an opportunity, don't quit, just keep going. Consistency is key, not perfection. Remember, you don't want to be a sideline Christian.

Take Your Bible with You as You Go

I have found over the years that taking my Bible with me has helped me start many conversations about God. I have opened my

Bible many times on airplanes, only to have the person next to me comment about the Bible and ask what I'm reading. I have been in coffee shops and used it as bait; just opening it up on the table seems to draw people in that are hungry for God. No other book looks like the Bible. It stands out and will let people know who you are and what you stand for.

If you go to school, walk down the hall with your Bible. If you work at an office, take your Bible to work and open it up in front of you while you are on lunch break. If you drive Uber or Lyft, put a small Bible on your dashboard. If you are a construction worker, take your Bible with you when the work crew is driving to that day's work location. No matter where you go, take your Bible with you and watch what happens. This is so simple; give it a try.

Wear Christian Clothing

Buy Christian clothing that boldly proclaims Jesus or even make your own. It's pretty easy these days to make custom T-shirts or other apparel. Our ministry just made a shirt for our TCU outreach that says "JESUS IS THE ONLY WAY." When you see someone wearing that shirt, you won't have to guess what they believe. I have found that wearing Christian clothing has helped me share my faith so many times, whether at Disney World, an airport, or a coffee shop. I have countless stories of people talking to me because of the shirt that I was wearing. As an added bonus, it will also help you get over the fear of man.

I love team jerseys and will wear them often. When I do, other team fans will start talking to me and make positive comments about the sports team I am representing. It's always fun to find fans that cheer for the same sports team. It is the same with Christian clothing. You will find that when you boldly wear apparel that talks about Jesus, other Christians will comment. It will show you that you are not alone, and your boldness will cause others to be bold as well.

Go to an Outreach Event or Conference

If you want a breakthrough in sharing your faith, then I want to encourage you to go to an outreach event or weekend training conference. You can read a book, watch a YouTube video, or even talk about what you have learned with others, but until you put action to what you learn, you will not begin to live it out in your everyday life. A level of accountability and community at these events can help you cross the chicken line. Some people have the ability to jump in without the encouragement of others around them, but that is not common. Personally, a weekend evangelism conference at our church started me living a lifestyle of outreach.

Many different conferences out there will train you in how to share your faith. I would recommend you find one that is not just teaching you to use a tool but also teaches you how to hear the voice of God and be obedient to what he is asking you to do. Tools are great, but tools without the Holy Spirit will leave you frustrated and are probably going to feel a bit awkward.

One of the best equipping conferences that I have been a part of is City Quake. My friend, Tom Ruotolo, is the founder of this four-day equipping event that has trained thousands of people and activated them in the United States and around the world. There are several each year in different cities around the US and in the nations. Get a group of your friends and go get activated together. You won't regret it, and it will change your life forever.

Get Equipped and Activated by 33rd Company

Do you have a call on your life to equip the church to reach individuals, cities, and nations? Does your church have a burning desire to turn its community into a mission field? Are you looking for ways to step deeper into a great commission lifestyle built around prayer, outreach, and discipleship? If you answered yes to any of the above, go to our website www.33rdcompany.org and check out the different initiatives and resources we have to equip the believer, to equip the church to reach the nations. This includes our Jesus Year, Full-Time Christianity Training, Make Disciples Events, Belong, and more.

All right, go do something today to be a part of bringing in the harvest that is ripe and ready. It's time to run!

GOSPEL GUIDE

LEAD WITH THE GOSPEL
ON OUTREACH WE LEAD WITH THE GOSPEL HERE IS A GOSPEL GUIDE TO HELP YOU GET STARTED
UNTIL SHARING THE GOSPEL BECOMES NATURAL FOR YOU.

CONVERSATION STARTER

HELLO MY NAME IS _____, I'M OUT TODAY LOOKING TO SHARE THE GOSPEL WITH PEOPLE.
WOULD YOU HAVE 2 MINUTES FOR ME TO SHARE THE GOSPEL WITH YOU?

HELLO MY NAME IS _____, WE JUST SPENT TIME PRAYING AT OUR CHURCH AND ARE NOW
OUT LOOKING TO PRAY FOR PEOPLE AND SHARE THE GOSPEL WITH PEOPLE. DO YOU HAVE A
MINUTE FOR ME TO SHARE WITH YOU?

HEY, I WANT YOU TO KNOW THAT JESUS LOVES YOU. CAN I PRAY FOR YOU IN ANY WAY?

TWO ENGAGING QUESTIONS

1. DO YOU BELIEVE THAT GOD CREATED YOU TO BE IN A RELATIONSHIP WITH HIM?
2. DO YOU BELIEVE THAT SIN HAS MESSED THAT RELATIONSHIP UP?

GOSPEL STATEMENT

JESUS IS THE ANSWER TO THE SIN PROBLEM. HE IS GOD! HE CAME FROM HEAVEN TO EARTH
TO MAKE A WAY FOR YOU TO COME INTO RELATIONSHIP WITH HIM.

DECISION

DO YOU WANT TO MAKE A DECISION TO FOLLOW JESUS TODAY AND TO BE BORN AGAIN?
IT'S IMPORTANT TO UNDERSTAND THAT SALVATION IS NOT ONLY A PRAYER. IT'S COMING INTO
A RELATIONSHIP WITH JESUS AND FOLLOWING HIM FOR THE REST OF YOUR LIFE.

JOHN 17:3 NKJV
AND THIS IS ETERNAL LIVE, THAT THEY MAY KNOW YOU, THE ONLY TRUE GOD,
AND JESUS CHRIST WHOM YOU HAVE SENT.

www.ingramcontent.com/pod-product-compliance
Lightning Source LLC
Chambersburg PA
CBHW051425090426
42737CB00014B/2826